SALVATION ON DEATH ROW

Salvation on Death Row

THE PAMELA PERILLO STORY

John T. Thorngren

All author proceeds from the sale of this book will be donated to
Patriot PAWS Service Dogs, 254 Ranch Trail, Rockwall, Texas 75032,
www.patriotpaws.org. Patriot PAWS provides service dogs
without cost to disabled American veterans and others with
mobile disabilities and PTS symptoms.

Cover and book design by Mark Sullivan

ISBN 978-0-9985216-8-8 (paperback)
ISBN 978-0-9985216-9-5 (e-book)

Printed in the United States of America

Published by KiCam Projects
www.KiCamProjects.com

To Christina, who has been with me from the start
and who has raised and provided for my son, Joseph.
I could never have kept going without her, or without my son,
who has been my rock. They are my earthly reasons for living.

Pamela Lynn Perillo

Pamela Perillo and I worked on this project from 2010 through 2017. The background for this collaboration is remarkable.

In the mid-1990s, a bid request appeared in our local paper for an independent firm to read the water meters once a month in an adjoining town. This job sounded like a perfect opportunity for "Jerry" and me to work together. Jerry lived nearby in the same neighborhood I did. He was smart, good with his hands, and unemployed except for odd jobs. And a big plus: I knew he would be trustworthy and reliable, not only from my own intuition, but because he was well-known and an avowed Christian who openly helped the homeless. He could read the meters, and I could supply a corporation, truck, insurance, bond, initial financing, and paperwork. A perfect match. After obtaining the necessary forms, I planned to approach Jerry with this idea, get his approval, and obtain a performance bond.

On a beautiful spring afternoon, I was fishing from the shore of a lake close to both our homes. A tree-lined bank about three feet high rose behind the shore where Jerry surprisingly appeared as if I had called him.

"Doinganygood?" he clipped.

"No, not really," I replied. After a few minutes of chit-chat, I made the proposal: your hands, my brains.

His response sounded like an electric typewriter, one word per stroke, far too fast for my aged mind to digest and not particularly on the subject. I tried to check the size of his pupils, but the sun was behind him, and I was unable to confirm my suspicion.

I had learned about looking for this pupillary phenomenon from years past when a young man came up to me while I was pushing a lawnmower, jerked it from my tightly held grip, and said,

"I'lldothat. Youdon'thavetopaymemuch."

That young man stared at me with dazed blue irises encircling little black ink dots for pupils. Pinpoint-sized pupils, I later learned, are one of the effects of speed (methamphetamine)—that and talking in a time warp.

Something didn't click at that point next to the lake between Jerry and me. Something was reminiscent of my conversation with the lawn-mower guy, so I let my offer die on the table. Jerry moved away shortly after that.

In 2010, about fifteen years later, I heard from Jerry's ex-wife that he had been tried for capital murder following a drug-induced rage that ultimately ended in several homicides. The state where the crime occurred, similar to Texas, used a bifurcated trial: one for conviction, the other for punishment. Jerry enjoyed an extensive rifle and pistol collection, including automatic weapons. This was, of course, brought out during his conviction and played a major part in his punishment. The jury returned a verdict of death by lethal injection. As of this date, almost twenty years later, Jerry still waits on Death Row in painful apprehension as his appeals twist through the court system, and the state scampers to find the necessary drugs for his death.

Does Jerry deserve the death penalty? I don't think so. Narcotics deserve the death penalty, but of course, one cannot separate the drugs from the person who uses them. Although the legal system has become more enlightened to the defense of mitigating circumstance in the punishment phase, nonetheless, Flip Wilson's famous argument that "the devil made me do it" doesn't seem to impress a jury. Prior to Jerry's trial, I, like so many others, was non-pulsed about applying the death penalty. Jerry's experience changed my thoughts and touched my life.

How many people have been touched by alcohol or drug addiction? An overwhelming number, almost two-thirds of our adult popula-tion. In my youth, the problem was alcohol. Somewhere in the 1960s, narcotics "exponentiated" as the predominant source for addiction. One of the key findings in a 2004 survey of 801 U.S. adults conducted by the Peter D. Hart Research Associates was: "Some 63 percent of U.S. adults surveyed said that addiction has had a great deal or some impact on their lives."[1] Certainly it has had an effect on my own family; a close relative passed away from a drug overdose. With such high probability that you, the reader, have been affected by addiction, let me pose a question to you. What if your loved one were so under the influence that he or she committed such an extreme act as that of Jerry or Pamela? How would you feel then about the death penalty? Not to pontificate or condemn, but another question: Are you under a dangerous addiction at this moment?

I wrote to Jerry, and we readily agreed to collaborate on his story in the hopes that it might help others. We had barely started before Jerry realized that because the penal system in his state (and all others) scrutinized every page of correspondence, the details of his life and the homicides could endanger his appeals. We placed the project on hold.

Still, the execution of someone who had been possessed by narcotics while committing a criminal act haunted me. As a fiction writer, the thought occurred: *The novel's the thing to place before the conscience of the people* (*Hamlet* paraphrased). Yes, a thought-provoking Great American Novel about the injustice of the death penalty, especially in my native state, Texas. I decided that my central character would be female. Midway through the novel, it was evident that I needed a description of the female Death Row Unit in Mountain View. On the Internet, I found an old prison pen-pal request from Pamela Perillo. After several letters and telephone conversations, Pam and I realized that we had the same purpose for sharing her story as that which Jerry and I had intended, a plan for a book born of a hope that it might help others.

John T. Thorngen

April 2, 2017

To: All held captive—in chains or addiction

I recently learned that the story of my life will be published at the beginning of next year. Toward the end of that year, I will have been incarcerated in the Texas Department of Criminal Justice for thirty-eight years. A few months after that will mark my sixty-third birthday, meaning that more than sixty percent (almost two-thirds) of my life has been in prison—a penalty for a brutal crime I committed under the influence of narcotics.

I still grieve for the families I hurt and pray daily for their forgiveness. After much research, the author and I located most of the members of these families, and I was preparing to contact them. Fortunately, before I did so, I learned that such contact is not permitted and can increase one's sentence.

This is a painful narration of my life and friends on Death Row. May you learn from it that experimenting with beginner and designer drugs is tantamount to Russian roulette. There is no *recreation* in recreational drugs. What happened to me could happen to you or someone you care about. May you realize what horrors lie on Texas Death Row. May you understand that no life is worth taking through a state-sponsored system in the name of revenge. May you see that we all have a purpose and are worthy of life, even in prison.

Pamela Lynn Perillo

Note Davenport, Iowa, as my birth home. Name me Pamela Lynn Walker. Set the third of December 1955 for my birth date, a day against a backdrop of cold, gray drizzle. With Christmas approaching, color me in a scene painted by Norman Rockwell set in America's Heartland—a Christmas baby, a precious cherub in a pink bassinet under the holiday tree, with wisps of auburn hair accentuating deep-water-green eyes looking into the joyous faces of her parents and siblings. Only Rockwell could capture the feelings of all those present, in their facial lines and especially in their eyes. My mother, smiling fully, beneath long brown hair. My father smiling also but with lips in a thin line, his brown hair slicked back, his sideburns just a hint. My brother and sister with varied expressions from a boy's questioning frown to a girl's happy grin.

But this is a misplaced dream, something I might have imagined from the cover of an old *Saturday Evening Post* resting atop knock-knees covered by a plaid skirt while sitting in a doctor's office.

By the age of ten, such ideas were mist upon the wind and resembled nothing of the muddy road I trod for so many years. Certainly, no joy could I remember in my journey from Iowa. As I grew older, I would learn that joy would look solemnly different from this misplaced dream. Surely infancy follows a divine plan to protect the memory of little ones. Sometimes I'm thankful for those very early years being blank slates of memory, for the brief time in my life before I was faced with all that would follow.

* * *

When I was a year old, we moved to California, the land of milk and honey. The family then was my father, Joseph Franklin Walker; my mother, Wuanita; my older brother, Randy; my older sister, Joanne, and me. Our portion of the land of milk and honey was an island called Compton in a sea of cities within LA County known collectively as Southern Los Angeles. Compton, one of the oldest cities in the United States, had by the mid-1950s become a mixture of warehouses, industry, and blue-collar residences, still mostly Anglo-Saxon. For my father, following better pay consisted of stamping out fenders for large trucks on an assembly line.

For a while, we rented a home on Peach Street. I don't remember anything about the house except the pretty name of "Peach" and that it was near El Segundo Boulevard. Besides, we didn't stay there long enough to remember much. Daddy evidently needed to move elsewhere. Perhaps it was a rent problem, or perhaps it was a neighbor, maybe a new neighbor Dad thought was the "wrong color." Minorities were moving in and were quickly changing the demographic to "less than one percent pure." But it might have been for a larger house; my brother, David, had just come into the world. Whatever the reason, we moved to another neighborhood in the city of Lynwood, several miles north and a smidgen closer to Los Angeles proper.

The Lynwood home was a real dollhouse and not much larger—an *Alice in Wonderland* variety. Although the ceilings were high, the walls kept closing in. A concrete stoop with one window to its left faced Cortland Street. There was no overhang at the front door to protect a visitor from inclement weather, but no matter, because it never rains in Southern California. From the outside, it was little more than an oversized shoebox, and on the inside, a child's diorama: a tiny living area on one side and a miniature dining room on the other; behind them two bedrooms, each wide enough for little other than double beds; a utility space designed to hold a washing machine; and a matchbox-sized galley kitchen in which we had to stand single file.

The bathroom is one of my clearest memories. To flush the toilet required quickly pouring a pitcher of water down its throat. The bathtub was an ancient, 1920s cast-iron relic with claw feet. On hands and knees, you could look under it and check for monsters, usually after the fact because they had already crawled into the tub and were trapped—huge, black spiders. On Cortland Street, at the malleable age of around five, certain events solidified in my memory.

"Ayeee," screamed Randy as he stormed in through the back screen door early one morning.

I was in the kitchen with Mom, who was standing at the porcelain, one-basin sink wearing her usual dress of nothing but a bra and panties. As we both turned, the reason for Randy's cries spilled like a red waterfall onto the checkered linoleum floor; crimson blood puddles jumped from the white squares and hid along the black. His lower lip wiggle-wormed down to the tip of his chin, a thin piece of raw flank steak.

"Thaf dog dif thif," he wailed.

"You're talking about King, the big German Shepherd down the street?" I asked. "He wouldn't hurt a flea."

"You were teasing him, weren't you?" asked Mom. "What were you doing to him?"

"A sthick. Pokin' him wit a sthick…"

"I told you not to do that, didn't I?" she yelled as she raised her hand to a striking position, retracted, and pressed a wet towel to Randy's face.

I heard Mom mumble some ugly words as she marched from the kitchen, words about not having time to waste in some hospital emergency room, needing some sleep, working at the restaurant at night to support us all. Minutes passed.

"Wenf is she comin?" asked Randy between sobs.

"I guess she's changing her clothes." Looking back on it, there might have been other things going on in that room, but one thing was certain, she was in no hurry to end Randy's suffering.

Randy never approached his canine adversary after that, but he sought vengeance in other ways.

Just a year later: "What do you call that little bird?" he asked me.

I was holding a fluffy yellow chick in my left hand and stroking its back with the other. "I don't know. I haven't thought of a name yet. Maybe 'Peeper.' Listen to her peep. Isn't she cute?"

"Let me see," he said as he grabbed the chick and in a blur plucked off its head. Blood squirted all over the back stoop as the poor animal fell to the ground, still wiggling. I screamed. Randy laughed. I didn't tell Mom. I might be the one who got in trouble.

There were other instances of retaliation against animals. Cats, neighborhood pets or strays, became Randy's victims of choice. They didn't fight back like dogs. Mom knew about it but didn't say anything. The first time I heard the shrill cry of a tortured cat, I ran out into the back yard.

"What are you doing?" I cried.

"Nothing. None of your beeswax." A small black-and-white kitten wiggled and writhed upon a clothesline, her ears "clothespinned" to the line.

The worst of the worst came around New Year's Day and the Fourth of July. A loud pop, followed by the wails of a wounded cat, and we knew that Randy had paper-bagged another cat with a firecracker inside.

Years later, I could come to understand Randy's behavior within the context of my family history. I would learn that abnormal aggression, especially with transference toward animals, can follow family lines.[2]

Certainly, a disposition to become addicted to drugs and alcohol is a well-known example of genetic or learned behavior within a family also. At that age, I had a gut sense that some things were very, very wrong, but it was impossible to put into context. Quite simply, this family life was all I knew.

* * *

Nearly always in her bra-and-panties "house dress," I guess Mom was what men called a "looker": long, brown, wavy hair (that she frequently combed while sitting at the dining room table), richly tanned skin, and distinctly green eyes. One would have thought her a native of

Malibu Beach rather than Iowa. Her beauty certainly worked for Dad; they added two more to the family while we lived in the dollhouse in Lynwood—another brother, Dale, and then my youngest brother, Ronnie.

My father was born in 1927. At the age, or should I say underage, of seventeen he enlisted in the military toward the end of World War II. Consequently, we always celebrated his *two* birthdays, his actual and the one he lied about in order to be of official age to serve his country. Although my sister and I would soon learn a very different side of our father, to most others I am sure he appeared to be a reliable man, slow to anger and a hard worker who did his best to provide for a growing family. Somewhere in Iowa, he received the nickname "Little Joe." I figured it was because all the Walkers are small in stature.

Even before Dale and Ronnie, the hope for peace and quiet from other family members was a mirage. After Dale and Ronnie came into our family, there were seven of us all together at Little Joe's mansion. I often thought of myself as Snow White living in a dwarf-sized house with seven dwarfs. Snow White in relation to the size of the house only; I certainly didn't feel significantly above the others in any other manner. The capacity limit for the kitchen was three, and it was fortunate that all of us were small.

Ronnie slept in a crib in my parents' room, but the rest of the children shared one of the house's tiny bedrooms, and three of us slept in one double bed. I usually slept at the end, across their feet, and awoke earlier than the rest. An ever-increasing twinge of emptiness reached down into my innards almost every night, a buried feeling that I was insignificant and worth so little.

"Why are you getting up so early, Pam?" asked Joanne.

"Because I need to."

"Your gown is wet. I can see it. Did you pee yourself?…I'm gonna tell Mom."

"Don't, Joanne. Just don't. You know we'll *all* get the belt."

My first day to begin school at Will Rogers Elementary was a rubber band of emotions, back and forth from happiness to dread. Breakfast was an upper.

"Oh, you're going to have so much fun. Meet new friends," Mom said with a fluorescent green to her eyes that seemed to tell me she'd be glad to see me gone.

"Joe," she screamed, "have you seen my sedatives? I left them right here on the kitchen counter. Doesn't anyone care that I've got to get some sleep before work tonight?"

* * *

As I walked to school, I kept telling myself: *You are pretty. You are pretty just like your mom. You have the same pretty skin, brown hair, and green eyes. You are going to have fun.* And the first day was great, especially recess. I was standing near the jungle gym when two girls approached.

"Hi," I said. "Want to watch me hang by my knees?" They giggled as I flipped my legs over the bar, and my dress fell down over my head. "We saw your panties," they laughed.

"My name is Ginger, and this is Renee. What's yours?"

"I'm Pamela, but everyone calls me Pam. I live on Cortland. Where do you live?"

"We both live on Duncan, right around the corner from you. We'll come see you after school. What's your address?" asked Ginger.

"No, no, no…We can meet at Logo Park just down the street, or I'll come see you….What's *your* address?"

My house was *visitors non grata*. It was fall and the weather was cool. We had no heat other than the gas oven in the kitchen. And the place smelled; it always smelled of something wet, something mildewing, something dead. And the commode, gosh, what if they had to go to the bathroom and find it took a pitcher to flush?

Renee and Ginger became my best friends at Lynwood, and I loved to go over to their homes and play. Renee even had a trampoline, but I sure didn't want them at my house—yet it had to happen at some point.

"I get to go first," I said at school recess later that fall as I held the tetherball and wound up to smash it around the pole.

"I get to play the winner," yelled Renee. Ginger lost. I was good; in anything athletic, I was good. After I had beaten Renee, it was time to go back inside.

"You've got oranges on the trees beside your house. I saw them on my walk to school this morning," said Renee. "Can we come pick some?"

"Oranges? Oh, we've got all kinds of trees. Yes, we've got two orange trees—sweet ones, nice and ripe. We've got peach, avocado, walnut, nectarine, lemon. Take your pick. You can come get some, uh…but you can't come inside. My mom's asleep. She works at night."

It wasn't exactly a lie; she did sleep during the day and work at night, but it was in the morning that she slept. Around noon, she awoke, took her happy pill, and combed her hair.

* * *

Winter was finally over, and the damp cold that permeated the house had evaporated into March. No more trying to stay warm from the oven in the kitchen. California is not always "the land of eternal sunshine." Winter does get chilly. March and the season of spring–summer–fall began—a season that changes little until the beginning of the next winter. Peach trees were blooming, crocus and tulips were flowering, and dichondra ground cover was flourishing. The annual uplift to my innate morbidity had arrived.

Mom had come home from work, fixed breakfast, and taken her sedative before closing herself in the bedroom. I was scrambling to get ready for school.

"Come on, Joanne, I've got to pee. You've been in there an hour. Open the door," I screamed.

"Bug off," she yelled back. Randy walked by and "frogged" me in the arm. "Ouch," I cried, and then Mom's bedroom door opened with a rush.

"I didn't do anything," I pleaded. "Joanne won't come out of the bathroom."

"Don't you kids understand that I've got to get some sleep? Get out of there, Joanne. All of you, turn around." A thrashing was eminent. Whatever was convenient—a belt, a broomstick, or a coat hanger— served as an instrument of passion. That day she chose a curtain rod. *A curtain rod?* Mom was not an old schoolteacher, but she thought in kind: If one of you is guilty, all of you are guilty.

That evening, after Mom had taken her upper to go to work, Dad and the rest of us crammed into the little living area around the fish-bowl-sized black-and-white TV. At Ginger's and Renee's houses were televisions that you could actually *see* while sitting in a chair several body lengths away.

The opening theme of *Bonanza* filled the little room like the water we poured into the toilet.

Dad loved Westerns. At the commercial, I asked him, "Does everyone call you 'Little Joe' because of Little Joe Cartwright on TV? You don't look like him. You've got slicked-back hair, and his is curly. But you always wear cowboy boots, blue jeans, and cowboy shirts. And your hair is brown like his. Is that the reason?"

"No," he said, smiling. "They've called me that ever since we lived in Iowa. I can't remember where it came from, but all my friends have always called me that."

"I'll call you Daddy Little Joe."

"Don't. Just don't."

I didn't yet realize how different they were. In that moment, my father was not unlike the handsome Little Joe onscreen with the wide, white smile that every girl loved, the loyal Little Joe who couldn't bring himself to hurt anyone.

CHAPTER 2

I was nine years old when Mom didn't return from work. Dad had come home from his job, and she hadn't been home all day. I remember him frantically calling all the local hospitals,

"Do you have a Wuanita Walker listed there? Wuanita *Tucker* Walker…Yes, I'll hold."

And he held on until she called two days later and told him she had run off with the cook at the restaurant where she worked.

From that point, Dad crumbled.

Perhaps Mom wanted more from life than living as the Old Lady in the Shoe who had so many children, she didn't know what to do. Divorce came quickly, and I never saw her again after that. Maybe, in hopeful retrospect, she would have contacted us eventually, but she and her new husband died in a car wreck a year later somewhere in the Midwest—Missouri or Kansas. I understand it was a bad crash. Fiery, a real mess. I would like to think she would have wanted to see us. I know a mother's bond with her children can go beyond flesh and bone. At the time, however, her absence only reinforced my poor self-image.

Similar to Randy's vendetta toward animals, Dad transferred his grief to revenge.

His first retaliation: "All right, kids. I want you to help me go through this house and find everything that belonged to your mother. Anything she left behind. Combs, lipstick, whatever. And especially any pictures. Put it all on the dining table."

The pile grew, and then from another room I heard the grating of a metal garbage can sliding across the wooden floor, a handle banging meanly on its side like a door opening and closing in a harsh wind. I walked into the room; a housefly crawled from inside the empty can and took flight. A whiff of some former garbage mingled with the seemingly ever-increasing stagnant smell peculiar to the Lynwood house. Wham, thud—the larger objects first. Everything we would have had to remember our mother by is buried in some Southern California landfill.

* * *

Mom and Dad were not heavy drinkers, but they sipped a few beers when they played Bingo at the Pike on Long Beach Pier. An outing to the Pike was like a breath of fresh, normal-family air. It seemed such a long way from Lynwood, maybe forty-five minutes, but an eternity when crammed in the back seat with four others—Randy forever punching me until I yelped and then Mother turning around to glare at me. Me, the cause of it all?

The Pike was another world, a man-made world neither on land nor sea but on wood planks suspended above the Pacific Ocean with hundreds of rides and amusement machines, even a gigantic roller coaster that rose high above the water. Sometime before I was born, they changed the name to Nu-Pike, but nobody ever called it that, just "The Pike." Mom and Dad would give us each an allotment of change, and we would head for the rides and the penny arcade. Dinner became whatever nourishment we craved: cold drinks, cotton candy, ice cream—all sorts of treats.

The ride back was always happy with recounts from everyone talking over the other, laughing.

"I almost got that watch this time," Randy crowed. "I had the tip of the giant claw right under the wrist band."

"That's nothing," said Dad. "I could have bought you a dozen of those kinda watches if I had just gotten a B6. One number! I had three ways to win, and the prize was fifty bucks."

"I got to ride the roller coaster in the front seat," I laughed. "And I swear when we were over the water, I know I saw a shark."

"You're such a ditz, Pam. It was probably just a dolphin," said Joanne, laughing.

Also, Mom and Dad never drank much at home. Maybe a few beers when friends came over for poker. But after Mom ran off, Dad took solace in the spirits, and certainly not holy ones. Little Joe would come home from work and set up his private bar in the dining room. Resembling a slow metamorphosis between Jekyll and Hyde, he'd cocoon himself in silence, staring out the front window while methodically imbibing red wine and inhaling Phillip Morris Commanders. I'd walk through occasionally to check on his progress. When sufficiently transformed, he'd mumble and laugh maniacally.

"Pamellas, sees if shum beer in the fridge…this shepo wine's burnin' my belly. Alls I c'n afford. Your mom's n'longer payin' her shhares."

And he chorused with a familiar, slushy laugh. The warning was out: "Avoid the dining room."

Almost overnight, the family went dysfunctional. Mom put the "dys" in it—walked away from us without a word and left a hidden hurt deep within me. Randy and Joanne tried to maintain the "function" that was left—and what Little Joe wasn't further eroding with his drinking. They did their best to look after the younger ones and maintain some semblance of order.

Relatives tried to help when they could, especially my maternal Aunt DeeDee. I wasn't there on the storied day she dropped by unannounced, but I heard about it. If I had been the worn-out fly on the wall, I think this is what I would have seen and heard: Little Joe was sitting on the sofa in the living room with Joanne on his lap. Aunt DeeDee walked through the front door without knocking just as Joe was fondling Joanne.

"What! What are you doing, Joe? You stop that right this instant."

"I…I wasn't…I wasn't doing anything."

"Don't lie to me, Joe Walker. I saw what you were doing. Joanne, go to your room and pack your belongings. I'm not letting you stay in this house for another minute, and as for you, Joe Walker, just be glad I don't call the police!"

"But…I wasn't…I wasn't doing anything…"

Aunt DeeDee and Joanne left for Kansas that same afternoon. Aunt DeeDee never returned to Lynwood.

* * *

By the time I was ten, Little Joe must have realized that he needed a sitter to look after the younger ones and me. He hired a woman named Helen.

I presume that Joanne's absence was the reason for me to become next in line for molestation. I was taking a nap one afternoon when I awoke to see Little Joe sitting next to me on the bed with a weird grin on his face.

"Stop," I screamed when I felt his hand between my legs.

I jerked away, ran into the bathroom and locked the door. Tears came quickly.

"Pam," he said softly through the door, "I promise I won't do it again."

"Cross your heart?" I sobbed.

"Yes!" But he lied. Shortly thereafter, he did it again.

Too much. It was too much on top of a mother's desertion and Joanne's departure. I felt totally betrayed, utterly unwanted by both my mom and dad. I had to confide in someone, so I told my girlfriend, Renee. She, in turn, told her mother, who reported it to someone at the PTA meeting later that week. This was the lead domino, the cue ball, the stirring stick in a man-made whirlpool. I was playing outside with my friends during the PTA meeting when I saw Little Joe and Randy drive into the parking lot, and I instinctively knew the story had come full circle. I ran between the classroom buildings and crouched down in the shadows on a blanket of ground cover, in what little green would grow there without sun. Randy found me.

"It's true," I cried. "He was touching me while I was sleeping."

"It must have been a dream, Pam. You said you were sleeping. Had to be a bad dream."

"No, I got up and locked myself in the bathroom. I couldn't have done that if I was dreaming."

"No, it didn't happen. Couldn't have. It was all just a bad dream," he said while shaking his head from side to side.

Perhaps the police agreed with the bad-dream theory. Although Little Joe was taken in for questioning, nothing happened. The molestation continued.[3]

* * *

Enough. It was enough to have suffered so many emotional upheavals and then to be treated this way by my father. I ran away. Anything had to be better. But I didn't last long as a runaway; the police picked me up and sent me to Los Padrinos Juvenile Hall in Downey, California, about six miles from Lynwood.

In Juvenile Hall, at age ten, I learned there was a way out. A large girl, a little older than I, asked me, "Have you ever done weed or drugs?"

"No," I replied quizzically.

"You need to try it."

"Yeah," another girl chimed in, "when you're high, your problems disappear. It's the greatest feeling in the world."

And so the seeds of thistle and rows of thorns were planted in soil ready to receive them and prepared to bear their bitter fruit.

Child Protective Services released me back into the custody of my father, and I returned to school. There, I approached the lower element, the older ones, those with a none-too-nice reputation, those reportedly doing drugs. Mary Swisher, who was already into the culture, became my best friend. And on a beautiful Saturday afternoon in the fall, at Mary's house, I had my first drug encounter.

"You sure your parents won't catch us?" I asked.

"No," she replied. "It's past noon; Mom is so boozed up, she wouldn't wake up even if the Russians dropped the A-bomb, and Dad is away on business. He's always away on business."

"Always away on business? Wow, I wish I had that kinda deal."

"Here, try a joint. It will get you in the mood. The boys are coming over shortly."

We both lit up. I was no stranger to cigarettes, and the girls at Juvenile Hall had instructed me on how to deep-drag and inhale it until you were about to pop. I overdid it and coughed. The room started rotating fast and then slowed. Dizzy and coughing and then giggle-silly. Everything Mary said was hilarious.

Later, after the party ratcheted into high gear, Mary offered me a red pill. I eagerly accepted it, and within thirty minutes I was flying. I could say anything; I could do anything; I was the life of the party and wonderfully in my element with *older* adolescents. I felt older and was eager to forget the childhood I never wanted. I would always gravitate toward older people.

With the abuse at home, I frequently ran away, only to have the police pick me up and send me back to Juvenile Hall. California Social Services eventually recommended that I become a ward of the state and be removed from home. By then, Little Joe had married Helen, our sitter. From that point until 1967 when I was twelve, I went from one foster home to another—eight altogether. All but two were abusive, and the two where I would have liked to have stayed were not acceptable to Social Services because I had become "emotionally attached." That was a no-no for a ward of the state who is not legally adoptable. (To my knowledge, my dad had not released his parental rights, nor had the state terminated them.)

The worst was the foster home in Paramount, California, which is another suburb of LA about six miles from Lynwood. *You pee that bed again and I'm gonna blister your behind.* I can still hear her threats through the halls of a bad dream, and not just threats but the sting of reality. And for a whole term of school, all she ever bought me were two dresses. Finally, I convinced the social worker to get me out. Whenever

I couldn't get Social Services to find another "home," I ran away, got picked up, and was sent back to Juvenile.

Los Padrinos Juvenile Hall in Downey became my home away from home, my sanctuary between horrors. The employees were like family. Mr. Step taught me guitar, and a lady in the kitchen, Ms. Jones, taught me how to knit and crochet. I had no idea what wonderful gifts these would be someday. I went to school there, and the science teacher let me take care of the iguana, a snake that ate goldfish, frogs, and lizards. A bizarre menagerie of creatures, but perhaps my chores satisfied a need to care for something when Little Joe and a dead mother apparently didn't care for me. I later wondered what the world would be like if God hadn't made animals, just humans and vegetation. In His wisdom that is beyond our comprehension, perhaps He made some of the animals just for our affection and comfort.

All the counselors and employees were my friends, and Super Chicken was one of my favorites. At the time, I didn't know why they called her Super Chicken, but looking back, it must have come from the Bible: "…how often would I have gathered thy children together, even as a hen gathereth her chickens under her wings…"[4]

"Pam, I know you haven't got anyone to visit you this weekend," said Super Chicken with a compassionate smile, "but I'll come and talk to you whenever I get a chance today."

She left a small sack of candy on the table next to my bed. The weekend visitors for the other children always bought little sacks of candy for them. Super Chicken knew hurt; knowing what I know now, she must have had some bad hurts in her life as well.[5]

Next I went to an all-black foster home in Lancaster, California, in the Mojave Desert some eighty miles from Lynwood. The distance from my former home to a new foster home was increasing; perhaps the state was running out of choices. A memorable experience: I was sick with tonsillitis but would not lie down to sleep. The house mom came in and asked, "What's the matter, dear? Why don't you go to bed?"

"I can't," I replied, "If I go to sleep, I'll wet the bed, and then you'll whip me."

"There ain't nobody gonna whip you here. I'll put some plastic over that mattress, and, Honey Child, you just go 'head and pee your little heart out."

Funny what a little compassion can do. I never peed a bed again.

Shortly thereafter, Mistress Puberty called, and what little was left of my childhood forever departed.

CHAPTER 3

At the end of 1968, I officially became a teenager. At thirteen years old, I climbed into the front seat of California's drug-coaster at the apex of Timothy Leary's "Turn on, tune in, drop out." It was a peer thing with little pressure applied. I needed closeness with others. I needed to belong. Drugs were readily accessible. The oldsters hadn't yet figured out the devastation they would bring to America.

My drug of choice was reds, one of the many street names for seco-barbital, or its brand name, Seconal.[6] Regardless of whether one called them reds or red birds, seggy, seccies, or Dolls,[7] they were simply *reds* to me—a bright chunk of fun-filled flame unknowingly borrowed from the very fires of hell itself. Being on reds allowed me to be what I wanted with my friends, to be one of them, to giggle and say bizarre things that they, being in their own false chemical happiness, would joyfully affirm. Yes, I was there. I belonged. And although there were those alarmist cries of addiction circulating, I knew it was just a rumor. Besides, I could stop anytime I wanted. I had proof: Namely, I didn't care for marijuana or LSD, and that *must* have meant I did not have an addiction.

In an odd arrangement during the spring of 1969, I was between foster homes and staying with Little Joe in Lynwood. Prior to allowing me to return home, there had been a family-counseling meeting at Los Padrinos Juvenile where Little Joe swore he wouldn't do anything. Besides, he had his new wife, Helen. I wasn't unduly worried. Helen was nice. I liked her.

On a Saturday night, my friend Mary and I walked the several miles from Lynwood to South Gate Park, a hundred-acre recreational oasis in another of the daisy-chain suburbs of southern LA County. South Gate, California, was angrily white until the riots of 1965 in nearby

Watts. After that, the demographic gradually changed to predominantly Latino, but even in the late '60s, it was still unwelcome turf for anyone but self-avowed Anglos. Likewise, the lowriders in South Gate that cruised the four miles of Tweedy Boulevard from State Street to South Gate Park were largely Anglo; Latinos occasionally queued in line but mostly preferred Whittier Boulevard some thirty minutes to the east.[8]

A gentle breeze carried a distinct smell from South Gate Park as we approached, and it wasn't that of azalea blossoms from the "Azalea City," the name South Gate adopted in the same year as the Watts riots. Besides, azaleas don't have a perceptible aroma.

"Like, what's that funky smell?" I said with a laugh.

"Yeah, heavy. Maybe they're burning some rotten leaves in the park," giggled Mary.

"Nah, people don't burn leaves anymore. Maybe they're burning Mary Jane's clothes," I said, laughing so hard that Mota,[9] the little puppy who had become my sidekick, jumped and pranced as if she thought it was a fabulous doggy joke also. Mota had recently joined the Walker family; a friend had given her to me as a six-week-old puppy, and she was a cute little ball of fur.

When we reached South Gate Park, I noticed more lowriders than usual. Their springs were shortened to the point that their frames almost touched the pavement, some of them hydraulically equipped to raise and lower the rear end or even the whole frame. In their low position, they slinked slow and low like jungle cats, ready to pounce. Normally, high riders predominated the Park area, hot rods and souped-up cars with their large V-8 engines, sporting lots of chrome trim. A blue-and-white Impala lowrider was turning around to head back down Tweedy. "That's Tom's car," I said as I turned to Mary, thinking it was a guy from school. "Tom!" I yelled. "Tom, wait." The Impala stopped and raised its rear up and down—slowly—as if to say, "Yeah, whadda ya want?"

"Oh, you're not Tom," I said, chuckling when the driver looked toward me. And what a look. He was the most handsome man I had ever seen in my life: beautiful mocha-bronze skin, and beneath his dark curls were see-through-you blue eyes, eyes that penetrated my heart and soul with a flash of lightning. His arm hung loosely out the window, every inch covered with tattoos—not the store-bought sort of tats, but prison-made with black ink, raw and real, a gorgeous sleeve. I can hardly remember what was said because my heart was throbbing too loudly, but soon we were all in his car. Mary and a male friend who happened to be standing nearby sat in the back, and Mota and I settled in up front with the handsome guy who introduced himself as Sammy Perillo.

"Let's go dancing," said Mary.

"Yeah, to the Pike, to the Pike, to the Pike, Pike, Pike" came a voice from lips I almost didn't recognize—from me, as if I were sitting in a balcony watching a big-screen movie in the distance showing a ravishing actor driving a blue-and-white Impala, an actor who combined the best of Paul Newman, James Dean and every other Hollywood hunk. My usual earthly detachment, induced by reds, was no longer my mood. Instead, everything seemed amplified. I gazed at the straight and meticulously curved lines in Sammy's tattoos, far better than those raggedy ones I had painfully endured in Juvenile.

As we neared our destination, the Pike, its ambiance and its smell of the sea brought back good memories. The night melted into dancing with Sammy in the Pike ballroom on a euphoric red cloud wet with liquor that we smuggled in from his car to mix with the punch. Sammy was on some sort of relaxed high—I could tell, even in my altered state—but I couldn't figure out what he was using. Must have been pills.

When we returned to the parking lot, Mota, who had been locked in Sammy's car, jumped with glee; her tail, which was twice the size of her little tan body, seemed to fill every window. But Mota had paid us back for her long confinement: doggy poop. Sammy was livid.

"Look what your damn dog did to my wheels, man...*Lurida cagna!* Filthy bitch!"

Words I've never heard before, many never together, and some that I assumed were Italian. Again I felt rejection, but after we had cleaned up the mess, Sammy cooled down, and we were back to having fun. After dropping the others off, he parked in front of my house and said for me to put the dog up and come back out. I watched him from inside for what seemed like half an hour. I wanted to go with him, but I didn't. I don't know why. Finally, he pulled away.

CHAPTER 4

Sammy Perillo was constantly on my mind after that first night. I wondered how I would ever be able to see him again. Then, one afternoon while Mary and I were hitchhiking along Atlantic Boulevard, a blue-and-white dream floated by: Sammy in his Impala. One might say, from this point, the rest is history.

My brother Randy enjoyed drugs, but not nearly to the extent that I did. His focus was on women, and at the time he was married to his first wife, Sandy. Mary was dating a boy named Terry. When we went out together, it was Randy and Sandy, Mary and Terry, and of course, Sammy and Pammy. Sammy and I became inseparable. Here I am as a young girl. If a picture speaks a thousand words, this one of me, I believe, says everything with only three: "Pammy's in love."

Pamela Lynn Walker, age 13

Like a Greek tragedy, I would do anything for Sammy. He was my focus, and the drugs, unfortunately, came with the package. Juvenile Hall, foster homes, drug rehab—nothing could hold me. I would run away from anything and anywhere to be with Sammy. Eventually, Little Joe and the State of California declared me an emancipated adult, under the promise of marriage to Sammy, and agreed that I would live with Sammy's parents. Sammy was nineteen. I was thirteen. I gave my little dog, Mota, to Dad, who'd liked her since she'd first arrived at his house.

One afternoon while Sammy and I were staying at Randy and Sandy's home…

"Let's go, Pam," yelled Randy. "Tijuana quickie marriages won't wait forever. Let's go before it gets too dark. Where's Sammy?"

Sammy was holding up our marriage. He had been in the bathroom for what seemed like an hour. I banged on the door. "What are you doing, Sammy? Let's go make it legal."

"Give me a few more minutes."

The doorknob to the restroom was worn and wobbly, with several different colors of paint crusting through chipped and grease-worn places. I tried it; it was locked. Below that was an ancient, yellowed-white faceplate with a large skeleton keyhole. I peeked through. Sammy was sitting on the commode and injecting what I instinctively knew to be heroin. When he came out, I asked, "What was in that syringe?" He mumbled, but I knew. All that time, I thought he was doing pills like me. No wonder he wouldn't take me out with his friends at night. Theirs was a drug bond to which I wasn't privy.

But for now, blissful marriage. So in the merry month of May we made the two-hour trip to Tijuana along the coast on Interstate 5. It was a beautiful night with sea-scented air blowing through open windows, and after a few reds, I was mellow, along with my husband-to-be, wrapped up in each other's arms in the back seat. In Tijuana, after we paid fifty dollars and filled out some paperwork, a man asked us in a thick Spanish accent, "Do you consent to marriage?" We both said, "I do," and that was it. If all we had to do was jump over a broom-stick, it was still good. It was official; well, almost—we never had it notarized in California.

With Sammy's heroin secret revealed, I soon made him shoot me up. My first hit on Satan's sweet syrup made me terribly sick to my stomach. But it didn't stop me; Sammy wouldn't take me out with his friends, and I knew this was the key—riding the devil's horse together. Thus began the "wonderful" days of spoons and needles.

By breaking and entering, shoplifting, and other petty thefts, Sammy, his friends, and I supported our habit. Sammy was on parole, and a dirty urine test landed him back at California Rehabilitation Center (CRC)[10] for eighteen months.

When Sammy was released, I, along with the other two-thirds of the trio—Randy and Sandy with Mary and Terry—picked him up at the gate. Per his request and certainly with no objections from us, we brought drugs with us. So much for rehabilitation.

* * *

We were cruising along El Segundo when I noticed Sammy nervously checking his rear-view mirror. He reached into his pocket and handed me a spoon, a syringe, and an empty balloon.

"Take these. If I get caught, they'll send me back to CRC."

I did as he said, not that I would ever do otherwise. We both knew that as a juvenile, I would get far less time than Sammy. Following the brief howl of a siren, the police curbed us.

"Miss Walker, you're underage and out past curfew. Would you step out of the car?"

"But I'm married to him," I yelped.

"I don't see any proof of that."

The officer grabbed hold of my right arm, tightly until it hurt, and pushed me into the back seat of his car. He tried to arrest Sammy on endangering a minor, but Sammy smooth-talked him out of it. And so, from time immemorial as Eve took the hit for Adam, who subsequently feigned innocence, I took the hit for Sammy, my beloved. As we drove to the station, I surreptitiously emptied my pocket of the heroin objects and tried to push them as far out of sight as possible between the back of the front seat and the corner post.

Shortly after being booked, an officer came in holding my balloon, spoon, and syringe. There was still cotton in the spoon with heroin residue.

"Pamela, we found these in the back of the patrol car."

"What makes you think they're mine? They could have been in there from the last person you pinched."

"Sorry, doesn't fly. We search the car after every arrest."

Once again I went to Juvenile, followed by a stay at the new Tarzana Rehabilitation Center. I ran away within a week.

Sammy was in a revolving door with incarceration. When he was absent during my fifteenth year, I was "forced" to experiment with other drugs since Sammy was my heroin purveyor and nurse practitioner all in one. Reds were still good, but I needed something stronger, something to distract me from the heroin I wasn't getting. Ginger, my friend from early childhood, was readily available to help me out. It wasn't heroin, but it was something totally different: the next trip, LSD.[11]

Ginger was in to the California hippie scene, so much so that the walls of her room were painted black and covered with fluorescent paintings. Black lights amplified the LSD effect. Hers was a perfect tripping room. It was also secluded; the entrance to her room was outside the rest of the home, and her parents left her alone.

That whole summer we tripped out on LSD, either in her room or surfing at Long Beach. We'd spend the day watching waves become animals and listening to the salt spray singing songs. At night, through the prismatic waves, a rising moon became a brilliant kaleidoscope of parrots and flamingos. Sometimes we'd stay at the beach all night and sit on the curb at five in the morning in front of Winchell's Donuts on the Pacific Coast Highway, laughing at the customers.

"Look at that guy in the green suit," I giggled. "Look at him chew. Wait, he's a giant frog munching a fly."

"And that woman in yellow," chortled Ginger. "I swear she's a rolling lemon."

To many a set of glaring eyes, we hysterically laughed the mornings away. But there was one instance of those trips that seemed prophetic. Years later, Ginger told me, "One time when we were tripping in my room, I saw a hatchet floating over your head. I heard it saying, 'This is a symbol of your death at a young age.'"

Toward the fall of that year, I tried another hallucinogen, something called cannabinol, intravenously, as injection was now my procedure of choice. Pills, alcohol, and marijuana were fast becoming little but tide-me-overs. The cannabinol was a white crystalline powder that we dissolved in a little water and heated in a spoon until it became a syrupy liquid.[12]

Although I never had a bad experience or flashback on LSD, this drug "came back" on me days afterward. I understand that the medical profession does not recognize it as a psychoactive drug, but nonetheless it happened to me. I admit it might have come from a combination of all the drugs I had been using.

One day, I was painting a small Buddha statue with fluorescent paint when I slipped into another dimension. The statue was holding a little girl and boy, one in each arm. They were crying, "Please help us." I jabbed at the Buddha; blood squirted from his head. An hour passed, then two, and I emerged in an eerie fog where I was poking him repeatedly with a paintbrush filled with fluorescent-red paint.

In 1972, at age sixteen, I became pregnant, and at the beginning of 1973, Sammy entered San Quentin Prison[13] on a five-year sentence for armed robbery of a Fotomat kiosk.

Shortly thereafter, San Quentin officially began its transition to a maximum-security prison, although Sammy was not in the league of violent offenders. In prison, he ran with the Aryan Brotherhood, as a matter of survival, and he always carried his membership card with him. Whenever he entered prison, his credentials appeared permanently engraved in black on the canvas of his skin: thunderbolts and Nazi symbols. And he had other tats to let everyone know his nature: a giant gorilla on his back, a hand holding a syringe on his stomach, the number 666 on his neck, the familiar scales of justice, and, of course, my name in several places.

I knew this baby would cement Sammy and me together. At five months into my term, when I visited Sammy, he would rub my belly and feel the baby kick. I knew he wanted this baby. This 180-pound handsome husband and I would become one forever, cementing our love through this child. I was still living with his parents, and they helped me kick the heroin habit. I had to do this for my unborn. It was brutal. I was sick for two weeks with chills and nausea. I couldn't eat, and what I attempted wouldn't stay down. Finally, I was clean. I wanted so badly to do the right thing, to be a good mother.

On the morning of February 4, 1973, I wakened with a feeling that something strange was happening inside me. A gray mist clouded the view from my window. Later, a cold drizzle followed. Perhaps it was the weather—I never liked the cold—but by late afternoon, I knew I was in labor. Sammy's parents drove me to St. Francis Hospital in Lynwood. The next morning, as the delivery process escalated, I screamed and hollered. I remember one of the nurses yelling back, "Hush, you aren't the only woman to ever have a baby." But I hurt, and so I screamed all the more. Finally, they gave me a shot, and I didn't wake up until the evening of the next day when a nurse touched my arm.

"Ms. Perillo, you have a beautiful baby girl."

"Ohhh…where is she?"

"She's premature. We are keeping her in an incubator. Would you like to walk down and see her?"

"I can't…I'm too groggy to walk. I can barely hold you in focus. Can't you bring her here?"

"No. You will just have to wait until you can *walk* down there," and she spun around to leave like a Tilt-a-Whirl starting up at the Pike.

"Wait, was it raining when she was born? They tell me I was born in the rain."

"No, not at all. Yesterday was one of those rare clear days when you could see the outline of the San Gabriel mountains. The rain the day before washed out all of the smog. It was a gorgeous day."

I remember mumbling something about good and bad luck and drifted off. Several days passed before I was able to walk down the hall and look at my baby through a big glass window. As the nurse rolled the baby's little cart toward me, the emotion became intense. I just stood there dazed, and then I started crying. All the tubes and wires connected to her faded as I beheld this precious part of me. She *was* part of me, and for the first time, I felt that this was something that belonged to me that no one else could take away. Such a treasured memory I will never forget. Sammy and I had already agreed on a name if the baby was a girl.

"If it's a girl, I want to name her Erica, after Erica Kane," he said.

"Erica? That horrible woman on that soap opera, *All My Children*? No way! No way am I naming my child after her."

Sammy finally picked Stephanie, and I chose Dawn for her middle name. Since she weighed just a little more than five pounds, she had to stay in the hospital for about a week or more. When I finally got to take her home, we stopped at Little Joe's house for a brief visit.

Pamela and Stephanie Perillo

Stephanie was a doll, the joy of my life, the culmination of all the hope within the darkness. I felt loved and needed. With dark, full hair and piercing blue eyes, she was the image of Sammy. I was fulfilled—a grown woman at age sixteen. Sammy saw her when she was just a few months old, and the light in his beautiful blue eyes confirmed all the love we shared in this healthy little girl.

"We are going to be so happy together when you get out," I told Sammy.

I call the photo below my "I have arrived" photo. I am standing in front of the house belonging to Sammy's parents, where Sammy and I were living. I am fulfilled. I am married. I have a child. I am all grown up at age seventeen. I am woman.

* * *

Pamela Lynn Perillo, Age 17

And then the proverbial *what goes up must come down*—my life bottomed.

On a foggy June morning while staying overnight with some friends, I awoke to one of them saying, "Pam, come quick! Stephanie isn't moving." I raced into the room where Stephanie was lying on her stomach in a makeshift crib. All I saw was her little hand extending from beneath her tiny blanket, and it was a sickening purple. I panicked. I frantically called my older brother, Randy. Shortly after, he arrived with the fire department.

As I was sitting on my bed, one of the firemen bent down and said, "I'm sorry; she's gone."

At just four months, Stephanie had died of sudden infant death syndrome (SIDS).

"How could a healthy child suddenly die?" I wailed.

That night, behind the closed door of the Perillos' bathroom, I took a large hit of heroin and slit my wrists. After this, events blurred into simple flashes of existence. I awoke in a hospital with a cast on my left arm. Three of my fingers do not work to this day.

The only thing I remember from Stephanie's funeral was kissing her cold lips goodbye. I took a picture, the last one with which to remember her. It is all I have left from her last stop on earth, my precious, darling little girl. Six months in a mental hospital did little to revive me from the bowels of depression and self-condemnation.

One of the hardest points was confronting Sammy, who was still in San Quentin. I knew his mood instantly when they brought him out into the visitation room. His blue eyes dulled and pointed at me like the ends of cold gray bullets in the chamber of a revolver.

"How could you let this happen, Pam? You weren't even home; you were partying, weren't you? What were you doing? Sleeping while our child died? How could you? This is all your fault. I'll never, never, never forgive you."

For an instant, my depression turned to rage.

"My fault! Wait a minute. If you had been there, then maybe *you* could have prevented it. But *nooo,* you had to get locked up for being stupid enough to do a robbery with a gun—right when I needed you most." And then the conversation turned even uglier, and my life followed an uglier road as well.

From that point on, all I cared about was shooting heroin. Like a bumper car at the Pike, I just bounced from one collision to another. Nothing mattered. Life, though precious to most, meant nothing to me. I rarely ever attended high school and never graduated. Soon arrested for auto theft and drug possession, I was back at CRC. After my release, I received seven years' probation and parole to a gay community halfway house in North Hollywood. There, I started shooting "H" again. I moved in with my friend, and we worked at the gay community center in Hollywood. But it didn't last. I left and just kept bumping along looking for a path where I could mash the accelerator to the floor and go faster than what the world had to offer. A dirty urine test put me back, one more time, behind the concertina wire of CRC.

After this release, a methadone program became a stipulation for parole. So the day after leaving CRC, I went to the methadone center.[14]

It worked and it helped. I started dancing at a topless bar and soon moved in with a girl from the bar. Methadone works, but just for those who truly want to kick the heroin habit. Praise the Lord that there is some help for those who try. To those who don't, methadone is like artificial sweetener compared to sugar. I started injecting heroin again with my roommate.

"Do you have any *stuff?*" I asked her on one of our nights off.

"No, I'll call our dealer." Her face brightened as she talked. "He's just got back from Mexico with some brown heroin and wants to try it out," she said, giggling.

We went to his place, where I volunteered to be the first, and when the brown syrup began to bubble in a spoon, he pulled it up into a syringe. It was warm and sweet in my vein, and then total blackness. After an eternity of nothingness, I awoke to a strange smell—raw garbage, a suffocating, summer-warmth smell of orange peels, egg shells, and coffee grinds. I was lying on my back, floating in a lake of cardboard boxes and other sharp objects, and I was completely nude. No shoes, nothing. Four green steel walls surrounded my little pool and opened into the evening sky where streetlights quickly told me my location. A Dumpster. I'd been tossed into a metal trash bin like so much rubbish. I climbed out and skittered into the backyard of a nearby house where I stole some jeans, a shirt, and a large sock from a clothesline. I used the sock for a belt. I jumped in front of the first car that came by.

"Where am I?" I asked somewhat belligerently.

"Why, you is in Watts," replied a demure, elderly black man.

"Can you get me outta here?"

"Oh, yeah. Yeah, you is right."

And the way he said it made me feel like he was glad to get rid of this single white dot in a black neighborhood at night.

Staying in the shadows where he dropped me off, I walked back to my dealer's place where my roommate had not yet left. When they opened the door, it was as if I had returned from my coffin in a weird set of grave clothes.

"You were dead," they both exclaimed.

"I tried everything to revive you, doll," the dealer said. "I stripped you and put you in the bathtub and, like, filled it with ice. You didn't budge. And you were turning blue. Well, like, you know I couldn't leave a dead body in my house…"

A turning point? A wake-up call to get my life together? One would think so. Instead, I used more and more heroin with methadone as a tide-me-over. I bounced between different dealers, and I kept putting off the payments to one of them. He kept calling and leaving notes on our door. One afternoon, I was standing in his kitchen trying to con him out of some more drugs when he charged toward me to make me an example to those who don't pay and play by the rules.

"I'm tired of your games, girly," he barked as he waved what looked like a small, black cap pistol. He didn't wait for a response; a small pop, and I felt the whiz of a bullet pass my ear as it headed out the kitchen window. My wanna-be gangster fortunately didn't have the proper fire-power, evidently only the proverbial single shell allotted to Barney Fife. He fumbled into his front pocket for another 0.22 bullet and began to reload. My swift, hard kick between his legs brought him to his knees, and I ran out the door. Maybe it hurt him enough that he left me alone. I don't know, but he never returned, and our business relationship, of course, ended. My girlfriend and I were now excessively into drugs, trying to tightrope that fuzzy strand between high and sickness. Then, out of the fog that surrounded me, Sammy reappeared.

CHAPTER 5

Once again, Sammy and I began anew at that point where incarceration had interrupted our syrupy dreams. Sammy and I would steal together, score together, and shoot up together.

Once more I became pregnant and was again on heroin, plus methadone. After Stephanie, the last thing I wanted was another baby. Abortion, of course, was an option, but something inside me would *not* permit it. Looking back, there could have been several reasons for my pro-life choice. Perhaps I didn't want the guilt of failure, or maybe it was fleeting inspiration from that old saying: "There's so much good in the worst of us, and so much bad in the best of us."[15] Many decades down the road, I am sure it was an angel planting a good seed within me as encouragement to go through with the delivery. I will always be grateful for that inner call.

I contacted my parole officer and asked for her help. She readily agreed to help me detox from methadone, perhaps because she thought I was clean and trying to make a new life. Although I was on heroin, my urine was always clean. It had to be; it came from someone else—sneaking in a bottle of clean urine long having been a ploy of the addict. Gradually, she reduced my methadone dosage, and I stopped the heroin. Again, I suffered the hard sickness of withdrawal, but with at least some consolation from the last time: I knew that it had an end and that my baby would be born without drugs in his or her system.

My older sister, Joanne, had moved back to California with her husband, and I was renewing our sibling relationship. I soon learned that her husband was a "macho" type who liked to beat up his wife to prove how tough and manly he was, and I often tried to keep her away from him.

One day during my sixth month of pregnancy Joanne stopped by my place and honked. "Hop in," she said as I walked out to her Volkswagen.

"Like, 'hop' isn't the right word," I replied as I slid into the passenger seat with my extended belly touching the dashboard. We drove to her house to check on her husband's whereabouts.

He was outside their house, spotted her, and headed toward his car. Once in his vehicle, he gunned the motor. In a moment, he raced ahead of us and forced her little VW bug into a ditch. As he roared onward, Joanne managed to spin out and U-turn in the opposite direction. Although we got away, my stomach squashed hard into the bottom edge of the glove compartment.

"Joanne, I just had a contraction!"

"How do you know?" she asked.

"How do I know? Of course I know. This isn't my first child."

"Don't worry; just relax and take some deep breaths," she said, which I did. And then, "I've had another! Great, I'm going into labor. Get me to a hospital."

St. Francis Hospital, where I delivered Stephanie, would not accept me because of a medical insurance problem (I didn't have any). So we went to Martin Luther King Junior General, the new county hospital nearby in Watts that had been built a few years after the riots. In the emergency room, a resident gave me a shot to stop the labor and checked me in for bed rest. Two weeks later, I went into labor, this time to the max, and delivered twin boys weighing two pounds each. At the time, I wasn't aware that twins ran in our family. When I talked to my father, he mentioned, "Did you know I had a twin brother? But he died in childbirth."

Sammy came to see his new sons and me in the hospital. "Those aren't my kids, Pam. They don't look nothin' like me. Who in the hell have you been with?"

"No one, Sammy. No one but you. How could you think otherwise? You've been in a cell too long. You're talking crazy."

Sammy left the room in a volley of curses, and I, never prone to tears, cried for hours.

I never saw Sammy again.

Years later I learned that Sammy had been sent back to prison, this time for a murder in Sacramento, receiving twenty-five years to life, presumably from the familiar "drug deal gone bad" scenario. Samuel Mario Perillo died in 2003. I don't know any of the details.

* * *

On the birth certificate for my twins, I listed the father as "Denied to State" and gave them my birth name of Walker. I told my dad that I would name one after him, Joseph Franklin Walker II. He said, "No, that won't work. I had a son that died who was the second, so yours will have to be the third." I had never heard of this before, nor of the fact that my parents had yet another child who died. So Joseph became the third, and I named my other twin Joel Steven Walker.

The fact that my father had been a twin whose brother had died must have been a bad omen, for twenty-nine days later, Joel died. I never got to hold him. I have since learned that twins come down through the female side of a family, that Little Joe and his twin came from his mother's side, and mine came through Wuanita. Nonetheless, I have always felt something prophetic about the death of Joel Steven Walker.

I took Joseph, the survivor, home with me—Joseph, the only good that came from Sammy and me.

I was still on a small dose of methadone when I gave birth, and right afterward, I requested a larger allotment. Soon I returned to dancing at Clyde's Nude Bar in Whittier, California. Whittier is another city some twenty-two miles from Lynwood. Never straying far from this area, and as a dog returning to eat his own puke,[16] I started using heroin again.

A girl and I shared a three-bedroom house. I had the downstairs and she, the upstairs. It was a good "working" arrangement: I danced at night, she worked during the day, and thus I was able to take care of Joseph. But there was little joy in Perillo-Land; I was atop the heroin horse with no way to dismount. "I'm a hope-to-die dope fiend," I bragged to friends and anyone else who would listen. "I want to die with a needle in my arm. *Oh, let me die with a needle in my arm*" was my mantra, a death wish that later turned prophetic down in Texas. Brashly spoken words often mysteriously gestate in the cavern of time to birth unimaginable monsters.

There was this old dude who frequented the bar where I danced, and he was always begging me to come home with him. I'd just laugh through a gag reflex. He did tip, and money is money. But one night shortly after another of his decrepit passes, I was sick and needed a fix badly. Two guys and I met at my dealer's house, and I suggested we rob this old man. We did.

The next day, the bartender at Clyde's told me the police were looking for me. I had also heard that they were driving around my neighborhood showing my picture to people and asking them if anyone had seen me. Not a surprise since the guy we robbed knew me. Stealing to support drug abuse does not require much gray matter.

I called my parole officer, and she wanted me to come in and see her. Yeah, *come into my parlor, said the spider to the fly,* and nowhere else except into a metal cage again, a place devoid of the heroin I so badly craved. While I was in semi-hiding, Mike Briddle, one of my co-robbers, called me from Tucson, Arizona, and said, "Hey, Pam, Linda and I are headed to Florida to elude the heat. Care to join us?"

"What's in Florida, Mike?"

"I have a friend there that runs a tattoo parlor; he'll help us. We're with this truck driver who'll pay your airfare to Tucson and give us *all* a ride. He just wants a friend and someone to talk to while we're traveling. He's got some good materials also."

Why not? I'd never been out of California, and through my drug-addled thinking, *I wasn't getting any younger—I was pushing 24.* Besides, the police were looking for me.

James Michael Briddle, Mike as everyone called him, was intelligent and soft-spoken. He was dark-skinned with thick, full Groucho Marx eyebrows. His eyes were like bottomless black caverns leading into the bowels of Hades. Mike probably never needed a gun for a robbery; all he had to do was stare at his victim. He had traits similar to those of Sammy Perillo, having served in CRC for grand theft and forgery. He was in San Quentin about the same time as Sammy, but I don't know whether they knew each other. They did belong to the same "fraternity," the Aryan Brotherhood, and had the same lifetime-membership tattoos. Whereas Sammy belonged to the Brotherhood for protection, Mike had a deeper relationship, thoroughly enjoying the fraternal parties where they kicked, bludgeoned, or "shanked" African-American or Mexican inmates. Mike's prejudices were monumental.

Linda Sutton Briddle, Mike's wife, had shoulder-length, brown, curly hair and average looks. She came from a wealthy family in Shasta, up in Northern California, an area totally distinct from Southern California. While a sophomore in college and earning good grades, Linda and several girls in the dormitory were reading a copy of *Easyriders* magazine,[17] a magazine dedicated to motorcycles and the wild side. An advertisement for prison pen pals appeared on a back page, and each chose an inmate. The purpose of their correspondence was never clear but appeared to be a self-chosen extracurricular experiment. Mike answered the letter that Linda had addressed to another inmate in San Quentin, Mike's frequent home away from home. Mike bragged about being a member of the Aryan Brotherhood and the fact that he had met Charlie Manson, whom he highly regarded. He further wrote that he knew he could duplicate Charlie's hypnotic power over others. After exchanging several letters, Linda frequently visited Mike, and she became his bride in a prison ceremony at San Quentin on June 12, 1979. She was twenty, Mike twenty-four. Conjugal visits could take place every ninety days. There were not many, because Mike soon got out, and Linda picked him up at the gates. Mike's braggadocio and Manson-mind-control personality drained Linda's spirit like a vampire and transformed Linda from a recreational drug user to a hard-core, intravenous existence. He taught her shoplifting skills and induced her to turn tricks to support their habit.

CHAPTER 6

I dropped eighteen-month-old Joseph at Little Joe and Helen's house. I wasn't worried about Joseph enduring any sexual abuse from Little Joe—he'd never bothered my brothers—and I knew Helen would be a good caretaker. So with the money Mike had sent me, I flew to Tucson, Arizona, to join Mike, Linda, and the trucker.

As we headed down the highway, Mike's ploy with the trucker became evident. I don't remember the trucker's name, so I'll call him Happy. Happy and I were supposed to copulate all the way to Florida as payment for my airfare. Later I learned that not only did Mike want me with him as insurance against my possibly turning him in, but also he and Happy had made this deal before I arrived.

I wasn't into that, and Mike and I fought many times over his belief that both Linda and I were placed here on earth to turn tricks and give him the money. The air brakes on Happy's mammoth eighteen-wheeler hissed as it shuddered to a stop on the interstate's shoulder.

"Out!" Happy yelled. "Get the *hell* out of my truck."

The moment Mike threw his duffel bag to the ground and slammed the door, Happy crunched gears in a rage and roared off into the morning sun.

After that, hitchhiking was our mode of transportation. It wasn't the best way to travel, and I was getting frantic: no methadone and no heroin. The winds gusting along the highways were cruel. I needed something warm in my veins. The sole substitute was pills that truck drivers gave us, and they were playing Ping-Pong with my mind. It had been several weeks now on the road without heroin. Traveling by one's thumb is slower than taking a Greyhound that stops at every ten-mile-apart town on a single-lane back road. After five days on speed and smoking PCP, we crossed the Texas state line. The last driver had sold us a long-lasting supply of PCP.[18] One of its street names is Angel Dust, but if it's the dust of an angel, it must be from the fallen angel, the devil himself.

And so we fell into the world of Texas. The state of Texas revels in being unique, the best, and the biggest, such as being the only state that has flown the flags from six other countries; the state that encompasses the King Ranch, a ranch bigger than the state of Rhode Island; the state that has the world's largest helium well; and the list goes on. Although no longer the largest state, Texas still claims to be bigger than Alaska after global warming melts Alaska's ice. When Texas can't be the best, then she will glance sideways and accept the last and the worst, such as a recent ranking at the bottom for health care and having the worst droughts in 2012, 2013, and 2014. Texas will never give up her cowboy-tough image. It is inherent in her history and in the land itself, from the water-moccasin-filled and mosquito-infested Big Thicket on her east to the powder-dry and rattlesnake-populated desert on her west.

Concerning crime and punishment, Texas historically reflects the toughness of her native roots. For the years 1976 through August 21, 2001, Texas had the highest execution rate in the United States at 472 deaths, almost five times that of any of the other thirty-five listed execution states. Although Oklahoma had a higher incidence per capita, Texas still ranked second in per capita deaths.[19] Texas had the largest prisoner population of any state, 157,900, at the beginning of 2013.[20] Certainly no hint of being soft on criminals should ever be cast on the Texas Department of Criminal Justice (TDCJ), nor on its governors with their seldom-if-ever-used powers of pardon.

Surely, unless one's mind were in an altered or *non compos mentis* state, he or she would not knowingly commit a crime in Texas. It is speculated that Charles Manson might have considered Texas as a home for "The Family" but changed his mind based on his experience of being arrested in Laredo in June 1960, for violation of his probation in California.[21]

Compared to California, Texas is indeed a tough state, a fact of which I was not aware and couldn't have comprehended anyway in my drug-addled condition.

Mike had a jail acquaintance in Houston "who would take care of us." Mike seemed always to know someone *who would take care of us,* so we thumbed it farther south, far out of our way to Florida, to the back side of Houston. Our truck driver needed to head even farther south and turned from Loop 610 onto the South Freeway near the Astrodome. Mike's friend was supposed to live near that point, so we walked back north from where he let us out up to Loop 610.

It was February 21, 1980, a Friday, and the weather was classic Houston, overcast and around sixty degrees, not particularly comfortable, especially when we stood near the freeway where two-ton bees and wasps zoomed by, flapping grit into our faces. When we neared the Astrodome, a van stopped in front of us on the shoulder. It was large and white with square corners like a bread truck. The driver, Robert (Bob) Banks, talked with us, or rather yelled over the traffic, for a few minutes and offered to compensate us if we would help him move from an apartment to his newly rented house. Money? We readily agreed. Mike's friend could wait.

Bob Banks motioned us into his van and insisted I sit up in the passenger seat. I glanced in the back and noticed a spider's lair of white nylon rope crisscrossing bedposts, tables, etc. After some introductions, Bob asked, "Where you all headed?…Florida. Oh, that's a great place to go."

"What do you do for a living, Bob?…The oil business…. I hear that's rather good pay."

"It's okay; at least it got me out of an apartment and into a house. I couldn't take all the noise and being crammed up together with others like bees in a hive. My new house is just a few minutes from here, over on Hepburn."

THE PAMELA PERILLO STORY | *43*

Like we knew or cared where Hepburn was; besides, Banks was making me edgy. He kept directing every question and response at my chest. Between his eyes on me and his glancing at the road, it was a miracle we even got to Hepburn. The street on which his new three-bedroom mansion rested was a single-lane blacktop in disrepair and close to a railroad track. The one remarkable thing was that there were some young palm trees along the road, palm trees just like those in California.

We helped him unload a few pieces of furniture and then returned to his apartment for another load. Because it was getting late, he decided we would resume work tomorrow. That evening, Banks took us out to a nice restaurant. We all waited behind him at the cashier's counter. He pulled a hundred-dollar bill from his wallet. I whispered to Mike, "He looks like he has a lot of money." Mike grunted and smiled in the affirmative. After dinner, we went to a bar. PCP and liquor were roiling in my head. I was not having a good time, especially since Banks kept sidling his chair up next to me and whispering sweet "uglies" in my ear.

"Would you please quit nuzzling me?" I groaned.

The party sort of died, and we left for his new home. After we slept that night, Banks treated us to breakfast, and we went to his apartment to shower and pick up another load of his belongings. While Banks was in the shower, Mike showed me what he found.

"He has guns. Look…and we know he has money. I'm going to call a friend back in California and let him in on this one. We got a bird's nest on the ground, a real live pigeon."

Mike made his call on Banks's telephone. His California friend wasn't interested. Mike placed the guns, a .45 revolver, an M-1 rifle, and a shotgun, into the van.

That night we went to a rodeo at the Astrodome with Banks paying our way. I planned on a good time; Western music, Western attire, and rodeos were things I grew up with and thoroughly enjoyed. I beefed up heavily on PCP and a few pills left over from who-knew-where and who-knew-what was in them. I guzzled plenty of beer at the rodeo, hoping it would dull the pawing and groping from Banks. When he left us for more beer, I said to Mike with a laugh, "I'd like to kill him."

Later in the evening, Mike left for a long time, and Linda and I went to find him. He was leaning against one of the walls in a walkway looking into space like he was in another dimension.

"What are you doing?" we asked.

"I'm planning."

"Are we going to do it tonight?" I asked.

He didn't respond, and we three returned to our seats, where Banks continued to prod me and talk nasty.

"Let's go. I'm getting really, really tired of this."

"No, baby," said Banks. "We're just starting to have fun."

"Mike," I said slowly and with emphasis, "we are going to do it tonight."

I don't think—but who knows what mind I had left to think with—that I was talking about anything other than robbery and getting away from this creep. We did *finally* leave and went to a bar where Banks continued his sexual onslaught. I continued to drink heavily.

* * *

Banks parked his truck in front of the attached garage at his new house, and we stumbled out, all grateful to leave the roar and bounce of his truck. I noticed a half-alive moon weakly trying to overcome the gloom that reflected the brightness of the Houston skyline. It was dropping into the 40s, a temperature I considered extremely cold. I noted a Volkswagen in the driveway.

Another Bob had arrived: Robert (Bob) Skeens. Bob Skeens, a friend of Banks from Louisiana, had just driven up to help with the move. Banks introduced everyone, and when he got to me, he leaped to my side and put his arm around me. I elbowed him hard. I walked over to

Mike and asked quietly, "Why don't we get a gun from the van and do it now?"

"No, it's not the right time."

I smoked some more PCP-laced marijuana, drank some beer, and got the .45 pistol. Angry, paranoid, invincible, seeing strange things, and feeling not myself, I had morphed into Missus-Mister Hyde personified.

"Linda, why don't you go get a gun from the van, and we'll come in and surprise them," I said.

I presume she declined. I faded rather quickly after that. But in the morning, the drugs and residual booze fought for what little sense I had left. I smoked another PCP-laced cigarette and got the pistol. Both Bobs had left to get coffee and doughnuts for their "guests." I woke Mike and Linda. "They're gone," I said. Mike, ever with an expressionless face, got the shotgun and hid in the hall closet.

When the unsuspecting pair returned, Mike rapped several times, quickly, from inside the closet. As Banks approached to investigate, Mike jumped out with the shotgun held chest-high and yelled, "Okay, this is a robbery!" Skeens responded appropriately in fear; but evidently, Banks thought we were playing a joke because he smiled and walked closer with his hands out and palms up. Mike hit him in the jaw with the butt of the shotgun and he fell. I came from the back with the pistol and a length of the white nylon rope from the truck and said, "This is no joke." I also had a machete that I used to cut some pieces from the rope for Mike to tie the hands of the dazed Banks. I pointed the pistol at Skeens and ordered him to the floor. Mike tied his hands also. We went through their wallets.

"Wow," he shouted as he flipped through Banks's thick pad of bills, "he's got 800 dollars here."

We placed Skeens in one of the bedrooms and secured his feet and hands to the bed. Mike sat down on the floor with Banks and looped the rope once around his neck. He motioned to me to grab the other end and pull.

Did Mike exert a Charlie Manson type of mind control over me? Did I think I was paying back Little Joe for his molestation? PCP mixed with everything else I had taken produced an altered state with demonic tendencies.[22] On PCP, there is no mind with which to think, just a dazed reaction to whatever happens.

* * *

Unlike hemp or cotton rope that when pulled tight remains in place, this was nylon, a fiber that stretches and gives. I guess this was the reason that later, the court determined—I don't know how—that strangulation took a long time, ten to fifteen minutes. I don't remember much, certainly not the length of time it took for what unfolded. At one point I was in a dark cave, Mike was a giant tarantula with glowing red eyes, and he was pulling me toward him with a bright-white spider web. At another point during a similar fog, Linda had evidently entered, sat down in front of me, and began to pull, because I felt the rope give for a moment. Through a bright tunnel, I heard thunder and saw her long, brown hair moving in a storm. Red rain fell all around her. She squealed and cried.

And then a voice echoed through moving darkness: "If you don't have the heart for this, then go load the Volkswagen," said Mike. "We're leaving in it."

Mike motioned to me to stop and go to the back bedroom where Skeens awaited the same fate. My memory contains total absence of that incident. All three of us methodically rifled the house for small items we could pawn, taking a camera and a radio/cassette player.

When we left, I felt the wrongness of all we had done in some deeply hidden crevice of my heart. That this was not me in my body. That I had to get loose from this high. That I had to get away from Mike and Linda.

CHAPTER 7

In the stolen Volkswagen, we retraced our hitchhiked entrance into Houston, heading back around Loop 610, the giant loop that circles the Bayou City. I suppose that the wise city council of every metropolis envisions a concrete moat around their perimeter to keep visiting traffic at bay. Usually, such happy circles end in just another gridlocked roadway in the path of progress as the city spills over the rim to seek its own level. Such is the situation for Loop 610, where noonday traffic yo-yoed forward at an infinitesimal speed. Where the Loop intersects Interstate 45, we turned north toward Dallas.

I was crammed in the back of the VW bug with my feet wedged in against the front seat and my back separated by only fabric and foam from the engine's puttering drone in the rear. I closed my eyes, preparing for a narcosis, a drug doze, but I couldn't get there. What we had done, to take the lives of others, was so bizarre, so intoxicating, and so stimulating—so amplified by the drugs—that it was all upon which I could dwell, and it was not pleasant. The weather was an ugly, cold-gray drizzle, the same that reportedly occurred on the day I was born, and yet whenever a ray of an outcast sun broke through the grunge, I heard opioid songs, a few pretty but most raucous and sour. My addled mind was in turmoil. This was not who I wanted to be.

Houston seemingly never stops its growth northward. Endless shopping centers and office buildings line multiple-lane, side-by-side highways separated by a continuous concrete barrier. Cars jockeyed for positions like NASCAR racers with inches between bumpers—rudeness with a vengeance.

"Look at that black S.O.B.," yelled Mike as a flat-bed truck driven by an African-American jumped in front, surely using the size of his vehicle to an advantage.

Were we not on the run, I suppose Mike would have stopped him for a little Aryan Brotherhood discussion, but instead Mike continued to drive like the proverbial little old lady.

As it neared noon, the eternal chain of urban growth dropped most of its links, and the highway split into a rolling two-lane with an island of green between ours and oncoming lanes. Tall pines dominated the island and also the sides of the interstate. Texas state troopers hid on little intersecting roads amongst the trees, the noses of their black Fords jutting outward like menacing, black spiders. An orange outline of the state of Texas bull's-eyed the sides of their front doors, black widows that suddenly sprang out to strike an unsuspecting speeder. Every time we'd pass one, or one would pass us, a vacuum sucked out all conversation and a chill reverberated in my heart.

Soon we entered the outskirts of Huntsville, Texas, and we all noted the tall, razor-wire-topped fence whose corner almost plowed into the right side of the highway at an oblique angle; a guard tower stood above the wire.

"I wonder if that's the state penitentiary," said Mike. "We need gas. I'm going to find out if it is."

At the next left-turn crossover, he drove into a filling station. It didn't take long to fill the little bug's tank, and we crossed back through the pine-treed island heading north.

"No, that's not the 'Big House'…that's what the attendant called it. That one is downtown; I've heard of it. It's the Walls Unit. It's where they execute prisoners."[23]

Peckerwood Hill Cemetery, near the Walls Unit [24, 25]

As we crossed over the median to head north again, Mike cocked his head to the right for a moment.

"That one we just passed back there, that prison jutting out near the highway, that's the Goree Unit. It's reserved for women…That's where you're going to spend the rest of your life, Pam." [26, 27]

I couldn't see his eyes, but I knew they were glinting with whatever sinister thoughts he had, those that one could never decipher in their emptiness.

"Ha," I laughed nervously.

Mike and Linda had been arguing since we left Houston, that is, ever since we saw buildings melting from the side of the highway. A little while after leaving Huntsville, their fighting had escalated into screaming and cursing. The air already thick with cigarette smoke became stifled with anger.

"Stop," I yelled. "I've got to have some fresh air…Why don't we split—right here—you all give me my share and let me out."

Mike arched the little VW bug off onto the shoulder and jammed it to a halt. Before it stopped rolling, Linda opened her door and jumped out for several yards. I pushed the seat forward, squeezed out, and ran into the middle of a nearby field. She trotted up next to me.

"Listen, Pam, he has the pistol and I'm afraid. I'm afraid he might use it...on either of us, especially me, if we tried to leave."

"Yes...I believe he would. I should have kept the pistol when I had it."

I resolved then that, eventually, I must get away from both of them. Two hours later, we arrived in Dallas. It was cloudy and colder, but no longer as gloomy. Asking directions whenever he decided to—certainly not when Linda barked at him that he was lost—Mike found the Greyhound bus station on Lamar. We circled it a few minutes until he ninety-degreed into a nearby underground parking garage.

"Leave the shotgun...I've got the rifle in my duffel bag. Just take what we can carry," he said softly. "And leave the windows open. Let the dust in so it will mask our fingerprints."

We walked up Commerce Street and into the main entrance of the bus station on Lamar. The entry featured an elongated greyhound in relief over the door. I gazed absently at this creature. I had always liked animals. And then it moved. I jerked my head down into reality and noticed a Dallas Police black-and-white parked out front, and then I remembered one just around the corner. This one next to me had an officer in it, and he glared at me. I grabbed Mike's elbow.

"Mike, there's a cop over there. They're looking for us...and there's another one on the other corner."

"Cops and bus stations—they're like refrigerator magnets. There is no way they could have found out already. Pretend you don't see them. Look straight ahead and don't make eye contact with anyone."

While Mike purchased our tickets and checked in his duffel bag, Linda and I sat in the waiting area, a crowded room with countless others carrying their belongings in various containers: paper sacks, canvas bags, and worn-out leather suitcases. Many were almost prone in their chairs, with their eyes closed, attempting sleep. The room was warm, body-heat warm, and stuffy with the smell of unwashed skin and a low-lying cloud of cigarette smoke that floated just above the heads of those standing, threatening to rain down tar and soot. "Where are we going?" I asked Linda.

"Who knows? Mike calls the shots."

Mike walked back from the ticket counter and sat next to me.

"We won't leave until around 7," he said.

"Why so late?" grumped Linda.

"Because that's when the bus boards, Linda. What am I, the dispatcher?"

As they got more into it, I went to the water fountain, took a chill pill, and left through one of the many doors leading to the buses. It was a giant garage with three wide lanes, three bus lengths deep. A half-dozen buses filled the lanes, some of them idling, waiting to start their appointed journeys. Each end of the garage opened onto a downtown, one-way street. Buses came in through one end and left through the other. Grating-covered holes, the mouths of large snakes, interspersed the dark concrete and swallowed black, melting icicles from buses arriving from the north. One grating near me was gulping down a spilt cup of coffee. Even with cold air slithering through the garage from the gray mist outside, the heavy stench of diesel fumes and dead oil burning squeezed the air from my lungs.

"I hate that stink," I mumbled. "At least inside the bus I won't have to smell it."

I went back inside, sat next to Linda, and gazed at one of the Greyhound emblems on the wall above the ticket counter—another out-of-proportion dog flying through the fourth dimension. I guess I dozed off, because I jumped at Linda's nudging.

"You almost fell on the floor, Pam."

"Let's get something to eat," said Mike.

In another large room, about half the size of the waiting room, we each ordered a steak, baked potato, and salad. Conversation was nonexistent. I tried to break the ice: "You know…we're eating on blood money." Linda looked upward and to her left. Mike stared at me, his classic stare of a thousand dead stars, black holes that spoke of nothing. Afterward we retreated to the waiting area. Then the now-familiar muffled, whining, monotone voice of the announcer bounced from the walls, saying again that one of the hounds was ready to run: "All boarding Greyhound service to Denver, Colorado, with stops at Fort Worth, Wichita Falls, Vernon, Childress…"

"That's ours," said Mike. "Let's go."

I don't remember much about the trip except that it was long, with stops in every town and an hour layover in Amarillo, Texas. I think I slept most of the way. The Denver station was similar to that in Dallas except the waiting area was larger and the tiles on the floor, smaller.

When we walked out of the Denver bus station, it was snowing. Mike motioned us into a cab.

"Is there an inexpensive place where we can stay?" he asked the driver. "I mean *real* inexpensive."

"Yeah, just a few blocks from here, a hotel on California Street."

The lobby we entered had all the trappings of being a "real inexpensive place to stay"—dim lighting and threadbare, grease-smudged overstuffed chairs and a sofa leaning toward one broken-down end. The few low-wattage light bulbs gave a warm, orange glow to a cozy area, a falsehood quickly exposed when one exhaled smoke without a cigarette. It wasn't much warmer than outside.

"No," I shouted, "this can't be." For there in the lobby, by trillion-to-one odds, were two of my brothers, David and Ronnie. "What are you two doing here?"

"We're just passing through. We have day work promised to us in Iowa. Why are you here?"

"Oh…just seeing the world. You know I have never been out of California."

Mike quickly wedged himself between us and turned on the charm. He was good at that, at talking eloquently, smoothly, and softly. I had a feeling that he was feeding his illusion of increasing a Manson following, his wanna-be-Charlie dream. (Unfortunately, my brothers received a large dose of guilt by association from their chance arrival here, especially since they remained with us until our departure.)

Linda got a job the next day at a nearby cafe. "We can use the extra cash," she said, but I felt that she got the job because she wanted to get away from Mike as much as possible. I could appreciate her position.

When Linda wasn't working, we scoured the downtown Denver bars near the hotel for drugs. One such excursion brought forth a demonstration of the other, less-than-sweet side of Mike, the side Linda and I tried to avoid. Mike had gathered Linda and me in a parking lot across from a bar on one of the streets that crossed California. "These *gentlemen* are going to get us some good stuff," he said, while never removing his glare from the faces of the two in front of him.

"Oh, yeah, dude, just give us the bread that we agreed on, sixty bills."

"And how do I know you'll deliver our Dillies?"[28, 29]

"Like, where we gonna go, man? It's in that bar, just a few hops across the street."

Mike handed them three twenty-dollar bills, and they hopped across the street, got into their car, and screeched off through a back exit. Mike imploded with a hiss and then exploded in a volley of curses. If he could have gotten hold of them, I am sure he would have pulled out their jugular veins with his bare fingers. Over the next several days, he silently dogged the area around the bar, hoping he could wreak his vengeance. If the thieves had been black, I am sure Mike eventually would have tracked them down and brought them to a slow and painful demise. I don't know if it bothered him so much about the rip-off or the fact that he was conned for somewhere near the same amount he got for selling the pistol to a patron in the same bar.

After a day or so into the beginning of March, I felt an overwhelming need to end this meandering, a turbulence of conscience, and a mother's yearning to get back to her son. I snuck down to the telephone in the lobby and called the Denver police.

"Yes, I want to confess to murdering two guys in Houston. There were three of us involved. You can find us at the hotel, me and Arthur Day, and his girlfriend, Sheila Davis...I don't know the name of the hotel, but it's downtown...What street? I don't know, but it's a big hotel; I think it's the Marriott."

Someone walked into the lobby; frightened that it might be Mike, I hung up the phone. All lies, but an opening cry in the dark. I just wanted to get as far away from Mike and Linda as I possibly could. I didn't like them from the start, and now they were unbearable. As I turned around, I saw that it was indeed Mike. From his hateful look, I knew he had seen me using the telephone.

"Who were you talking to?"

"I...I...Listen, Mike, I'm tired of this place. I don't like the cold. I never have liked cold, and I want to leave. I want to go with my brothers to Iowa. We've got relatives there, and I'd like to see them."

He reached for the telephone, jerked it from its cradle and hit me on the side of my head.

"If you leave, I promise you that I will kill one of your brothers. Would you like to pick which one now?"

I walked rapidly away. I knew he would do what he said.

The next day, in a state of desperation, I trudged around downtown Denver. Denver was cold. Black snow-slush clung to parked cars and clumped in piles along the gutter. When snow lies in new birth as I saw it in a blanket covering the field of a nearby ballpark, it is pretty. When it dies on a city street, it turns ugly. I noticed a patrol car stopped at a traffic light and knew it was time. He turned with a startled nod when I knocked on the passenger-side window.

"My friends and me killed two people in Houston."

* * *

The next morning, I signed a twenty-six-page confession condemning Mike and me and exonerating Linda, not that it mattered under Texas law or the law in most other states. If five people are involved with one person who shoots another, they are each as guilty of homicide as if each of them had pulled the trigger. They continued to question me even after I signed the confession.

"I'm curious," said one of the detectives, "why did you confess? Houston Police had no suspects at all. You could have stayed on the lam for at least—oh, I don't know—maybe another week." And he smiled as if he had told some sort of joke.

"I'm tired of running, and I want to see my two-year-old son."

The Denver Police immediately arrested Linda and Mike, along with my two siblings. I have always felt that they traced my phone call from the day before, because I never told them where we were. My kin were, of course, quickly released having solid proof that they weren't anywhere near Houston in February.

Linda and Mike opted to delay the inevitable and fight extradition. I didn't. I wanted as far away as I could get from both of them. However, with the normal legal proceedings involving any extradition, even an uncontested one such as mine, I didn't leave Colorado for two months.

On April 30, I left for Stapleton International Airport, handcuffed to an Officer West, and we boarded a plane to Houston Intercontinental Airport. Things were moving fast. Shortly after we were airborne and not climbing an invisible hill, I said, "You know, the confession I gave them in Denver isn't the truth. Actually I killed them both. By myself. Mike and, of course, Linda had nothing to do with it."

He nodded slowly. "We'll take care of it when we get to Houston," he said.

This was a spur-of-the-moment ploy because I did not want Mike or Linda to come back to Texas. I wanted rid of them for good. But it was a naïve ploy of youth and guilt.

In less than three hours, we taxied into the Houston airport. Houston Intercontinental, renamed George Bush Intercontinental years later, is some twenty-plus miles north of downtown Houston. We rode in a patrol car along Interstate 45, the same highway on which I had left, but we didn't exit on the infamous Loop 610. We headed straight into the heart of the city, to the Harris County Jail, my new home for months to come. After being searched, re-searched, and assigned a cell, they sat me in a little room with Officer West, several hardened-looking men, and a stenographer. I told them again that I was solely responsible. Sometime later, they asked me to sign the new confession. I didn't. By then, prudence had digested the fruits of stupidity.

The Harris County Grand Jury had already handed down an indictment, in absentia on March 5, in the 248th District Criminal Court, of capital murder under Section 19.01 of the Texas Penal Code:[30]

> …while in the course of committing and attempting to commit the robbery of ROBERT BANKS [Robert K. Banks, Jr.-Texas Death Certificate], hereafter styled the Complainant, intentionally caused the death of the Complainant by strangling the Complainant with a rope.
>
> It is further presented that in Harris County, Texas, PAMELA LYNN PERILLO, hereafter styled the Defendant, heretofore on or about, FEBRUARY 23, 1980, did then and there unlawfully while in the course of committing and attempting to commit the robbery of BOB SKEENS [Bobby Glen Skeens-Texas Death Certificate], hereafter styled the Complainant, intentionally caused the death of the Complainant by strangling the Complainant with a rope.[31]

Although I was indicted for both murders, the prosecution eventually charged me just for Skeens. My arraignment occurred on May 5, and I met my two court-appointed attorneys, Robert R. Scott and William W. Burge. In Texas, the court appoints two attorneys for the indigent in a capital case. Remanded to the Harris County Jail without bail, I awaited my "right to a speedy and public trial" as required by the Sixth Amendment of the U.S. Constitution. It was soon in coming.

CHAPTER 8

After leaving the courtroom from the indictment, my attorneys and I met in a small room where they told me that the Harris County District Attorney's Office would seek the death penalty.

"The death penalty?" I swallowed.

"Yes, we have a new district attorney, Johnny Holmes, and he seems to show no mercy in capital cases."

I felt as if I were lashed to a bull in a stampeding herd of cattle—no control, all voices and events taking place in another dimension, a surreal experience. They tried to comfort me, but I was just a balloon in a breeze, slowly floating away, unattached.

For several months, the legal system played out its script of motions: a motion to dismiss, a motion to set aside, a motion *in limine*. Both the defense and the prosecuting attorneys agreed to have me psychoanalyzed. I assumed the defense was hoping for a position of mental incapability and the prosecution, for no such possibility. As if I were a frog in a biology class, my brain was examined at Ben Taub Hospital for over a month. From a long list of foreign-sounding words, the single phrase I remember from one of the psychiatrists was "currently suffering severe depression." Yes, I suppose you would call it depression. I was terrified, and I was alone. I had committed a brutal crime, and I was looking at death in a foreign country called Texas. I was never a violent person. I had never committed a violent act. How could this have happened?

They started me on 150 mg of Elavil[32] twice a day (a total of 300 mg) and 5 mg of Valium.[33] At least I could sleep, and that is *all* I wanted to do. The drugs dulled the filth and smell of the Harris County Jail on Franklin Street, a facility that must predate the American Revolution. Sewage seeped down the walls all the way to the first floor.

Whether from broken lines or upset inmates stopping up their toilets, I don't know, but I do know the sewage produced a population explosion of "Houstonian" cockroaches. The Houstonian cockroach is a nonevolving, prehistoric monster. Compared to a buzzard, this cockroach is just as large, and like a buzzard it can fly. Woe to anyone in its flight path. It attacks, clinging to your clothes and necessitating a repugnant, hands-on grip to rip it off, but the most repulsive act is having it land in your hair. Velcro™-type legs, all six of them, tie square knots in every surrounding strand of hair. Pulling this nasty bug out takes great strength and great intestinal fortitude not to hurl. Creepiest of creeps, however, is to step on one. Ugh! A crunch that can be heard cells away followed by a squish and a cupful of orange-yellow goo.

While taking the "antidepressants," I didn't hear those roaches that occasionally landed in the toilet, went for a swim, and made the sound of surf hitting the piers of the Pike in Long Beach, California—a lifetime away. Some call them water bugs, which makes you think of a graceful underwater bug ballerina. What a euphemism. They only like filthy water.

Voir dire (jury selection) started August 4. Selecting a jury took eleven days, far longer than the trial itself. An officer escorted me to the Harris County Criminal Justice Center, a giant skyscraper several blocks from the jail. The court never saw me in handcuffs or jail attire, clothing that might bias a jury. Inmates could buy makeup from the jail commissary, but with no money whatsoever, I borrowed from others who helped me to look like anything but a criminal, and the secretaries of my attorneys lent me dresses.

Still groggy from antidepressants, I rode the elevator to the sixteenth floor, to the 248th Criminal District Court. Entering the courtroom was like stepping out into a noonday sun from a darkened room. Intense fluorescent lighting bounced unmercifully from blonde-paneled walls. We sat down at a large table reserved for the defense; the prosecution had its own table, sort of like two forts ready to wage war. I dozed off but awoke quickly when the bailiff boomed out as Judge James entered, "All rise. The 248th District Court is now in session, the Honorable Judge Jimmy James presiding. Be seated, please."

Since watching *Bonanza* on TV with my dad, I've always enjoyed Westerns, but this was surreal. Lawyers, the D.A., assistant D.A.s, so many men were wearing cowboy hats and boots. They spoke in a foreign dialect. My ears could only understand the fast-clip, amplified up-and-down song of the Californian language. These people spoke in a soft monotone like cold syrup straining to leave a bottle. If there were any melody to a sentence, it started high and fell like stones in a well. I half expected the judge to raise his robe and withdraw one of a pair of holstered six-shooters and lay it next to his gavel.

And the judge's name? Jimmy? I understand that this is a frequently given and recorded name, especially in Texas, but at the time I thought it peculiarly similar to movie cowboys such as "Hoppy" or "Gabby." The district attorney was most notable, a Wyatt Earp persona with a handlebar mustache as wide as the horns on a steer. It was a scene from a bad Western, and when they started questioning prospective jurors about their having any qualms about my lethal injection, I knew they were out to lynch me.

The Harris County attorney general with the intimidating mustache was John B. Holmes, Jr. He was the interim replacement for Carol S. Vance, who resigned before the end of his term in 1979. Had Vance remained and been re-elected, it is speculated that the D.A.'s office might not have moved for the death penalty. This is conjecture, of course, but it should be noted that Vance was both the son and grandson of Methodist ministers and noted to have become involved in the evangelical Christian ministry during his later years as a prosecutor.[34] In 1996, Carol Vance, then chairperson of the Texas Board of Criminal Justice, asked the state to create a Christian faith-based prison program at the old Jester Unit outside of Houston. This prison later officially became the Carol Vance Unit.[35]

After his interim appointment, Holmes was re-elected for five more four-year terms, evidently satisfying the citizens of Harris County and their desire to get "tough on crime." Holmes was quite aggressive in seeking the death penalty in capital cases. Researcher Scott Phillips[36] notes that during the period from 1976, after the U.S. Supreme Court reinstated the death penalty, to 2008, Harris County, if it had been a state, would have ranked second in executions in the nation after the state of Texas itself. This period covered all but three years under Holmes. Phillips made a study of 504 defendants indicted for capital murder during the period of 1992-1999. Of these, Holmes sought the death penalty for 129. Numerically, there was no racial bias: approximately equal percentages for the death penalty for whites, Hispanics, and blacks. However, statistically, the death penalty demanded for blacks was much higher for "less serious" forms of murder (as defined by Phillips) and much lower for all groups when the victims were black victims rather than white. This study, an Issue Brief, showed no discernible differences between white and Hispanics.

Holmes's position on applying the death penalty appears to follow Pontius Pilate's wash-my-hands doctrine.[37] Holmes claims to care little about his critics and thinks much of the criticism that comes his way should be directed at the people who make the laws: "It's your business if you criticize the death penalty. But I think you are out of line if you are being critical of me." Instead, Holmes says death penalty opponents should focus their fire on legislators. "I have never stumped for or against the death penalty," he explains. "That's a legislative issue. It's a personal issue that's wrapped up in morality and religion. I've looked at all the issues that are important to me. And I've resolved it in my heart and mind. I've resolved that I'm doing what I'm supposed to do."

On Holmes's behalf, former Assistant U.S. Attorney Andy Horne wrote, "Holmes was a hard worker and always—always— in the office before 8 a.m. John Holmes' attitude [toward the death penalty] nonetheless is correct—legally speaking: Legislatures make and change the laws while the Executive branch, including the District Attorneys, enforces those laws. It is no criticism to enforce the law aggressively. It is a violation of the oath of office to do otherwise."[38]

One incident during the pre-trial barely caught my attention. Little did I know at that point that it was the insertion of a thin piece of silk in my tapestry by the Master Himself. The prosecution was questioning Mr. John O. Vennard, a prospective juror, or in legalese, a "venireperson."

"Mr. Vennard, would you be able to render the death penalty should the facts in this case clearly warrant such a judgment?"

"It would be very hard for me to give a person death. Nevertheless, I would be able to sit on a jury that returned such a verdict," he replied.

"So, you are saying that you could render the death penalty in the punishment phase of this trial? Let me read you the three clear-cut questions that each juror must answer in the affirmative to render the death penalty as taken directly from Article 37.071(b) of the Texas Code of Criminal Procedure:

IF the defendant's conduct that caused the death of the deceased was committed deliberately and with the reasonable expectation that the death of the deceased or another person would result;

IF there is a probability that the defendant would commit acts of violence that would constitute a continuing threat to society;

IF raised by the evidence, whether the conduct of the defendant in killing the deceased was unreasonable in response to the provocation, if any, of the deceased.

"What I am saying is, number one, did the defendant expect that the deceased would die from her actions? Number two, if ever released, would the defendant continue such acts of violence? And number three, was the conduct of the defendant unreasonable to any provocation from the deceased. If you can answer yes to all of these three questions, then you must render a judgment for the death penalty. Could you, if evidence so presented itself, answer yes to these three questions?"

"I don't know whether I could find a person guilty of capital murder and answer the questions affirmatively, but I will certainly try to fulfill this responsibility if selected. Yes, I could reach a fair verdict, including a verdict sentencing the defendant to death, but that would depend on the facts and circumstances."

"What you are saying, Mr. Vennard, is that you would examine each of the three questions meticulously for a potential negative response?"

"Uh…yes."

"You think that you might have to answer one of this questions in the negative?"

"Yes, I am pretty sure."

"You are saying that you would be more than likely to answer one of these questions with a definite no, am I correct?"

"Uh…yes, I would always answer one of these in the negative so the defendant could receive life imprisonment rather than death."

"Regardless of the facts, you would answer one of these in the negative."

"Uh…yes."

"Your honor, we challenge this venireperson for cause."

"Mr. Vennard," said Judge James, "before I rule on this, let me ask you as simply as I can put it: Could you return a verdict for the death penalty?"

"No, I would avoid giving the death penalty…Well, if the facts were horrible enough, I *guess* I could give the death penalty. It would be a more severe penalty."

"Mr. Vennard, let me repeat my question; could you return a verdict for the death penalty? Yes or no, *please.*"

"Uh…no."

"The court grants the prosecution's challenge for cause. Mr. Vennard, thank you; you are excused."

"Your honor," said one of my defense lawyers, "we would like to examine Mr. Vennard."

"No, sir," said the judge with an air of no equivocation and no room for rebuttal. And thus Mr. Vennard became, in a reversed sort of manner, an "angel unawares."[39]

* * *

Prisons, hospitals, funerals—any place where human misery exists, you are likely to find a dedicated Christian attempting to bring comfort. When those in the ministry learned that the D.A. was going to seek the death penalty, various volunteers, including graduates from Teen Challenge, visited me. They ministered to me; I went to church services; I listened to Bible readings, but other than a desire to hear more, there was no booming voice from the heavens, no lightning, no blinding light.

Karen Apple often came and talked to me in the Tank (the name given to a room in the Harris County Jail with cells around the periphery holding from one to three prisoners). Karen had a background in drug abuse and found cure and conversion in Christ through Teen Challenge.[40] She had a marked influence on my redemption.

Another person who visited me was Levita Henley, a Harris County volunteer jail chaplain. Levita would come and spend the whole day with me, sitting on the floor outside the bars of my cell and talking to me. Levita was a mighty messenger, a Pentecostal, with no hesitation in her commitment to Christ. We talked for several days, and then she read Bible verses to me. During the trial, she had me recite the Sinner's Prayer with her:

"Dear Lord Jesus, I know that I am a sinner, and I ask for Your forgiveness. I believe You died for my sins and rose from the dead. I turn from my sins and invite You to come into my heart and life. I want to trust and follow You as my Lord and Savior. In Your Name. Amen."[41]

This particular Sinner's Prayer is from Billy Graham's 1954 London Crusade. I am sure these were not the exact words; there is no standard format, no formula, and no prescribed incantation. The leader of the prayer, often referred to as the messenger, opens their heart to and turns their mouth over to the Holy Spirit. The receiver opens their heart to commitment and receives each word into their soul. If not recited with a repentant spirit and an open heart, the words fall on rocky soil and fail to grow.

The words of this prayer with Levita fell on fertile soil. When I repeated "Amen," I felt something throughout my whole being—physically, emotionally, spiritually—a change in my very blood flow as if I were a new person, light and free of the weight of incrimination. That night, however, I struggled to accept the free gift of redemption. *How could God forgive me? How could He ever turn His back upon the horrible crime I had committed?*

* * *

After my jury selection concluded, my trial began on August 19. Once again I rode the cramped little elevator reserved for the accused to the sixteenth floor of the Harris County Criminal Justice Center, the 248th District Court. I was extremely sleepy. They had given me an extra dose of Valium for the trial. I don't remember whether the elevator ride took a minute or a day.

In an anteroom, the officer removed my handcuffs, and I straightened a new dress. Procedure requires that a female defendant wear a different dress each day of the trial. Thus I entered the courtroom as a "normal" person with makeup, dressed in "normal" clothes rather than that of an already condemned villain, pale and in chains, wearing an orange jumpsuit. That was presumably the idea.

Mike and Linda Briddle, my co-defendants, were not present during the trial, neither for the defense nor for the prosecution. Almost six months had passed, and they were still fighting extradition from Colorado.

The conviction part of the trial took a little more than a day, a sort of formality, I suppose, since I had pleaded guilty in Colorado. However, Texas and several other states where the jury decides punishment require a trial for conviction so the jury can hear the details of the case. And details did they hear. The prosecution read my guilty plea into the record, all of its twenty-six pages with emphasis and examinations on every gruesome item from corroborating crime-scene personnel. During the conviction phase of my trial, and also in the punishment phase, I kept nodding off because of the Elavil and Valium. One of my attorneys would kick me under the table, and I would jerk to attention like a startled deer—giving everyone the obvious picture of being rudely awakened and that I was bored beyond remorse and just didn't care.

I left the courtroom on August 20, not sure the jury could render the death penalty in the punishment phase that started the next day. I covered myself with prayer late into the night.

The punishment phase of the trial took about the same length of time as the conviction. The prosecution again brought out the gruesome details of the crime. Every time they mentioned California, they pronounced it with the connotation of Sodom and Gomorrah, referring to it nasally as if the very word had an odor reflecting the liberal thinking and prominent drug culture so prevalent in *Caleefonyuh*. They brought in the old man that Mike and I had robbed in Whittier. It didn't occur to me that he might—just might—have been looking for revenge against the young girl who had spurned his sexual advances. Then they read and entered my complete juvenile record from California:

"At age eleven, on October 13, 1967, Ms. Perillo, then known as Pamela Lynn Walker, was declared a 'runaway' and referred to the Department of Public Social Services. She was placed in two different foster homes by Protective Services.

"At age twelve, on December 29, 1967, again she was declared a runaway and referred to probation.

"At age twelve, on March 19, 1968, once again a runaway and referred to probation.

"And again on March 22, 1968, she was picked up as a runaway. Note this: she ran away five times in less than six months.

"Finally, the court docket caught up with her three weeks later, and at age twelve, on April 4, 1968, she was declared incorrigible and made a ward of the court and subsequently placed in a foster home. It did not take her long to be picked up as a runaway again, on May 15 of the same year. She is twelve years of age and has been picked up as a runaway on six separate occasions in just the space of seven months— *only seven months*. Able to adjust to rules? Able to obey the law? Ladies and gentlemen of the jury, do you see a pattern here? And it gets worse."

How can it get any worse? I thought. *How can running from an oppressive environment be considered such a terrible crime?*

"Ladies and gentlemen, on February 2, 1969, she was arrested on a petty theft charge, was counseled and released. It's starting to go downhill now.

"On July 17, 1969, again she was picked up as a runaway minor." And he continued with three or four more of the horrendous charges of runaway and curfew violations.

"When Ms. Perillo reached the age of fifteen, we see the 'incorrigible' label she received at age twelve starting to manifest itself in more egregious criminal arrests. On March 19, 1971, she and her friend Mary Swisher were arrested for DUI in South Gate Park being high on 'reds' and violating curfew.

"Still but fifteen years of age and on March 31, 1971, arrested for selling 120 capsules of Seconal to a state narcotics agent. And just four months later on July 6, she was arrested for possession of barbiturates. Ladies and gentlemen of the jury, it keeps going on.

"At the ripe old age of sixteen, on March 1, 1972, she is arrested for possession of drug paraphernalia and being under the influence of heroin."

All the other incidents seemed a blur to me, but that one I remembered. That was the one where I took the rap for Sammy.

"And finally, the last arrest record from California, the last conviction before this one here in Texas for *murder*, on July 20, 1973, Ms. Perillo, now age seventeen, was arrested for possession of stolen credit cards. Of course, we already know about her warrant for theft in Whittier when she left that state for her transgressions here in Texas. If you were to plot a timeline for the severity of her criminal acts, you would see a steeply rising curve. I hope you will remember all of these facts when you answer the second question in rendering the death penalty, that you should do so, specifically in the *positive*, 'If there is a probability that the defendant would commit acts of violence that would constitute a continuing threat to society.' Thank you."

There was no one to testify on my behalf: no friends, no family member, no one to state that this was *not* the sort of act that we would have expected from a young, naïve girl who had never done anything violent in her entire life. I never heard what happened to Ronnie and David after they were released in Denver. Ronnie was a juvenile, just sixteen, and a runaway. Was he returned to California? I don't know, but if he were, I know now that he didn't tell Dad about me. Not that Dad or Helen could have come; they didn't have the money. I was alone.

The jury returned the death penalty the next day. I understood later from media interviews of the jurors that much of their decision hinged on the fact that there was no one there to speak up for me.

I was stunned, walking around in an Elavil fog and not able to comprehend. Shortly after that, I insisted they take me off the Elavil. I needed a clear head to absorb the enormity of what had transpired. Once again—definitely for the last time—I went through drug withdrawal. Sleep was elusive, especially when I was worrying about a Houstonian cockroach crawling across my face.

Soon I would transfer to Huntsville along a now-familiar Interstate 45, past the ever-creeping tentacles of the expanding city of Houston, past the pine trees on a median-divided highway and into the Goree Prison Unit for Women, the place prophesied by Mike Briddle where I was to spend the rest of my life—ironically to await my execution to end the rest of my life. Perhaps not only the words from oneself, but those of others, are so powerful in manifesting reality.

CHAPTER 9

Even after the trial was over and I had already received the ultimate punishment, I had to wait a week before they transferred me to Goree. We left at midnight in a car with two detectives in the front; I was handcuffed in the back seat. The hour-long trip was devoid of conversation except, occasionally, between the detectives: work-related or trivial, certainly nothing to engage my contribution. I felt like I was some animal headed to market—inarticulate, uncommunicative, just so much meat. They were large men with white shirts and poorly tailored sportscoats that failed to hide the bulges of their shoulder-holstered Colt revolvers. I assume they were Colt revolvers because, after all, Texas felt like a foreign land from out of the Old West, and the .44 Colt revolver was the gun they used in the movies.

Gradually, the officers defrosted and brought me into the conversation. They even stopped and bought me breakfast. As I wiggled awkwardly out from the back seat, one of them, the one with the shortest hair, unlocked my handcuffs. "Ms. Perillo," he said unsmilingly, "if you try to run, you understand that we will have to shoot you." *Like where and why would I run? I was a naïve twenty-four-year-old kid in a surreal world.* The breakfast was good; the Elavil withdrawal had subsided, and I could eat and sleep again.

At the Goree Unit, I was searched repeatedly to the point of absurdity. Where and what would I find to hide on my person? After being documented, I was handcuffed and led to my cell. The Death Row section was at a lower level, in a dungeon-type atmosphere. It was at the end of a long hall housing prisoners on Administrative Segregation (Ad Seg).[42] Presumably, Ad Seg is not meant for punishment, but one would never convince a prisoner otherwise. At the end of the Ad Seg cells, a red-painted board crossed the concrete floor and identified the last three cells in a row as those reserved for the Death Row inmates. Linda Mae Burnett was in the last cell. I was in the first, with the empty cell between us. My cell could not be next to an occupied one because of an automatic, mandatory ninety-day suicide quarantine as required by the prison system. I suppose an empty cell between us was as close to a quarantine as they could get.

I learned that Linda Mae Burnett was allegedly a co-conspirator with Joe Dugas in the murder of Dugas' in-laws. In return, Joe was going to help murder Burnett's ex-husband so she could receive his Social Security. Joe could keep the $50,000 life insurance proceeds. This part of the conspiracy did not occur. Linda shot four of the adults among Joe's in-laws. Joe shot a child. All of them were murdered execution style at a pre-dug grave. Joe bragged to his brother shortly afterward, and the brother then related the event to the Vidor, Texas, police. Linda was convicted and sentenced to death by lethal injection. She entered the Goree Unit at the end of 1978.

A television hung from the ceiling next to the bare wall across from our cells. Linda had fashioned a coat hanger so she could reach it and turn the channels. Thank goodness, or we would have had to watch soap operas on Channel 2, ad nauseam. It was an exceptionally dark period in my life—in every aspect of the word.

Physically dark. The walls were a dull, concrete-gray and there was no light in my cell. Not that we needed light during the day since multiple fluorescent bulbs flooded the hallway. Trying to watch TV required mental blinders to focus on the picture. A barred window on the back wall allowed the barest of diffused light through an opaque material during the day, with nothing visible or distinguishable outside. At night, dulled lights encased in round, thick glass outlined the interior of my cage in a dismal, yellow gloom. Only the flickering of the TV produced any useable light, sometimes accompanied by an occasional violent lightning storm that might add a stereo effect through the murky window at the other end of the cell.

Linda had seen on a TV newscast that I was Death Row-bound and therefore headed for Goree, so she saved up and bought me two Zero® candy bars. As a treat one night, I decided to eat both of them. I had finished one and was halfway through the other when a bright flash from the television lit my cell, revealing every detail of the remaining half-eaten candy bar. White worms were wiggling outward, some whole, some severed, and I immediately gagged and threw up. I was sick for days. Poor Linda, I know she tried; however, a lot of time had passed between my sentencing date and when I ate the candy bars. Also, I would not be surprised if they were wormy from the point of purchase. We have always suspected the lucrative prison commissary and vending business to be a tightly held family affair where low quality and high prices were well-known kin.

Mentally dark. Death Row inmates were confined to our cells 23/7 and allowed outside—alone—for just an hour a day in a little area they called the Rose Garden. The Rose Garden was to the rear of our cells behind the windows we couldn't see through. It was a small fenced-in area with rose bushes around the perimeter. A round, white table with an umbrella in its center sat in the middle of this area, and two opposing chairs welcomed the inmate and any of her imaginary friends. The scene reminded me of the proverbial palm tree on a marooned island. Oh, so welcome, however, was this one precious hour per day to feel the sun's warmth and to breathe air that didn't carry the distinct waft of concrete and steel. Even my bed was steel, bolted into the wall and covered with a thin piece of padded, lumpy blue plastic for a mattress. No chairs, no furniture, nothing but a sink and a steel toilet—comfort was not in the Goree Prison vocabulary. And the icing on the cake: My birthday came and went while I sat in a cage of emptiness and despair.

Spiritually dark. But there were glimpses of light. I knew I was with God but felt like I was standing in the front yard of His house looking through an open door but not strong enough or not welcome enough to enter. *How could He forgive my unspeakable act?* My soul was in turmoil, and I was floundering in waves of angst. Levita Henley, the saint who led me to Christ, often came to visit me. She repeatedly told me that I must forgive myself before God could forgive me; to do otherwise was refusing His gift of grace.

Levita is a Christian, often called a two-by-four believer. Although this expression gives one the impression of a faith that is hard and unbending such as a 2-by-4-inch board—and rightfully so—it comes from the Bible, the Book of Acts, describing the miracle at Pentecost. Specifically, it is found in Acts, chapter 2, verses 2 through 4, and hence the 2-by-4 reference. In the upper room, the description in verse 4 is the crux (NIV): "All of them were filled with the Holy Spirit and began to speak in other tongues, as the Spirit enabled them." Then after Pentecost, in further describing the Acts of the Apostles, Paul questions approximately twelve disciples as to whether they had received the Holy Spirit since they believed. Acts 19:2–6 (NIV): "...and asked them. 'Did you receive the Holy Spirit when you believed?' They answered, 'No, we have not even heard that there is a Holy Spirit.' So Paul asked, 'Then what baptism did you receive?' 'John's baptism,' they replied. Paul said, 'John [the Baptist]'s baptism was a baptism of repentance. He told the people to believe in the one coming after him, that is, in Jesus.' On hearing this, they were baptized into the name of the Lord Jesus. When Paul placed his hands on them, the Holy Spirit came on them, and they spoke in tongues, and prophesied." (These verses, 2 through 6, conjure up an even larger and stronger board, a 2-by-6-inch board, frequently used for main beams and rafters). From these passages, most 2-by-4 believers consider salvation to be a two-step process in which the gift of speaking in tongues is proof of full salvation.

I tried to speak in tongues like the melodious language that Levita used, but it just would not flow. One night as the TV's light flickered through the bars, I crawled under the cantilevered iron slab of my bed and pulled the sheets down for a tent. "Lord, please accept me; please let me speak in tongues. Please, *please* give me the gift of tongues so I know I am saved." Nothing came forth but "Uhh…Ahhg…Erugh" My eyes poured so many tears upon the concrete that I could see puddles growing like those during a rainstorm. A mélange of radiating TV colors penetrated the end-flaps of the sheets and bounced from these pools but never colored the surface beyond silver-black. Dark and deep waters. I was defeated.

I know that Levita's unyielding conviction in the gift of tongues was God-purposed, for it encouraged me to read more and seek spiritual wisdom. I now know that He, the Holy Spirit, gives many other gifts in addition to speaking in tongues.[43] Often, it takes time in our Christian walk to realize our gifts and where to apply them. I know mine now, and I find peace in their presence.

* * *

Prison life is regimented and monotonous, but there are changes, and even small changes, good or bad, are welcome. At the beginning of 1981, I moved into the cell next to Linda and we could talk. Silence may be golden, but not so when you can't speak to another person for excruciatingly long periods. We also could spend our one hour per day together in the Rose Garden. She was about seven years older than I, thin, quite attractive with dark, shoulder-length hair. She wore glasses. Linda and I talked about our children (she had three) and about how she had made peace with her Maker.

Many on Death Row seek salvation, but not all do. And I believe the negative term "jailhouse religion" would have no meaning to someone condemned to death. A prisoner who has jailhouse religion is often considered to be one who professes salvation in Christ Jesus but is only seeking special favors or an early parole. Although I am sure there are some who do so for personal gain, I believe many of them have been tragically mislabeled.

In this photo, you can see me after leaving my ninety-day (three long months') isolation and having doubts about my salvation.

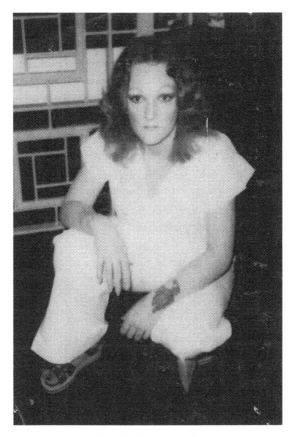

Pamela Perillo, 1981

Later in 1981, TDCJ converted the Goree Unit into an all-male population and transferred the female Death Row to the Mountain View Unit in Gatesville, Texas.

The state established the Mountain View Unit in 1962 for serious offenders (maximum security) formerly at the Gatesville State School for Boys. Mountain View operated separately from the Gatesville State School for Boys, which dated to the late 1800s. In 1971, a class-action lawsuit on behalf of juvenile offenders instigated major changes in the Texas juvenile justice system. Judge William Wayne Justice ordered the large juvenile penal units to disperse and place the offenders in smaller and separate units. Gatesville closed in 1979 and Mountain View in 1975. Mountain View became the Mountain View Unit for Women and, as noted, acquired the female Death Row in 1981.[44, 45]

Warden Lucile Garrett Plane made some changes to the cells reserved for the female Death Row at Mountain View; she removed the bed slabs attached to the walls and replaced them with beds with springs and a real mattress. She painted the walls light yellow and added a small wooden desk and shelf. Warden Plane began her service in the Texas criminal system in 1970; she became the first female warden in Texas at the newly transformed female prison at Mountain View. Linda and I could crochet afghans and make pillows. Since we could move our beds around the cell, we would place them next to the window and cover them with our cell-made pillows to resemble a daybed. Warden Plane allowed us to hang pictures. I had lots and lots of horse pictures on my walls. They reminded me of my love of animals, and horses reflected my fondness for Western movies shared with my dad.

There were six cells at Mountain View, three on each side of the hallway, and each cell had a window from which you could see outside. Mine opened onto the rec yard (recreation area). Every bit twice as large as the Goree cell, this was a welcomed change. Like Goree, Death Row was at the end of a hall with a TV mounted for each row of cells to watch. A crash-gate (a locked gate across the hall) set these cells apart from the others.

The recreation facilities consisted of a day room at the far end of the hall near the officers' control area and an outside yard. Unfortunately, it was still available just one hour per day. In the day room, we could watch TV and play Ping-Pong, dominoes, or Scrabble. In the yard, we could play volleyball, horseshoes, or croquet. Volleyball had always been one of my favorites growing up, so when others joined me later on Death Row, I always tried to get them to play.

In the fall of 1982, Linda Burnett had her trial reversed on appeal. The court had wrongly allowed introduction of a tape made during hypnosis, an act that violated her attorney-client privilege. A year later in her second trial, the jury gave her life imprisonment. I was now the only female on Death Row in Texas and looking at possibly becoming the first female executed since the mid-1800s, a dubious honor often delegated to Chipita Rodriguez.[46]

With Linda Burnett no longer with me on Death Row, I had a lot of time to think, to reflect, and to express in verse.

Here is a poem I composed:

Brick and Steel
Pamela Perillo

We walk into this place
Broken and bent
With our heads bowed low
We had no idea
What all of this meant
As the cloud begins to lift
And our feelings come back in tune
We slowly look around us
At our new life we are
Beginning
In this one little room
From a world without boundaries
Where your dreams
Reach the sky
To the same incessant question

You ask over and over
"WHY"
Our world is stripped of color
Turned to brick and steel
As we look around and realize
It doesn't matter
How we feel
We now answer to a new name
With a number on our back
We watch people come and go
Along with fear
And sorrow
Too
Never quite knowing
Exactly what to do
We no longer have a choice
Of what goes on
In our lives
That choice has been
Turned over
For others to decide
We pay for our mistakes early
Baring them each and every day
I will never be able
To forget this
There's absolutely no way
Our hearts begin
To put up walls
To shield us from the pain
Either we fight for
Everything it's worth

Or we bow our heads in shame
Some of us choose
To keep our feelings
To fight for what we have left
Instead of handing them over
Like a possession
They have kept
You may hold my body in chains
But my soul
You will never claim

Several months after my trial in August 1980, Linda Briddle, Mike's wife, relinquished her fight against extradition from Denver in a plea bargain arranged by her lawyer, Jim Skelton. The State of Texas offered Linda the opportunity to plead guilty to non-capital murder, which meant that the death penalty would not be a consideration. Jim Skelton declined this plea, however, and Linda accepted her return to Houston based on two counts of aggravated robbery after Skelton pointed out that Linda was not involved in the homicides per my confession in Denver.

Jim Skelton was a well-known prosecutor who later went into private practice as a criminal attorney in Houston. He defended David Owen Brooks, who confessed to being present at the sexually motivated killings of twenty-five to thirty boys by Dean Corll and Elmer Wayne Henley, Jr. in Texas during the early 1970s. David Owen Brooks received a life sentence.

At Linda Briddle's trial, Skelton argued that all the blame belonged to Mike Briddle and me. Skelton cited our criminal records and described us as being of a different ilk than Linda, who he said came from an educated family and had accidentally become mixed up with Mike through some sort of bizarre sociology experiment during her college years. Skelton described me as "heartless and without remorse," a plausible impression during my trial since I was somewhere near comatose on Elavil and Valium. Neither Mike nor I testified at Linda's trial, but Skelton presented degrading photographs of us alongside "beautiful-people-type" images of Linda.

The jury bought her clean-background defense and sentenced her to five years' probation. Linda returned to California to serve her probation and had her marriage to Mike annulled in April 1981. In July, she married again and became Linda Fletcher. Jim Skelton kept in close contact with her and traveled to California to the wedding to give the bride away. She is often referred to in court documents even prior to her second marriage as Linda Fletcher rather than Linda Briddle (I assume as a means to distance her from the crimes).

Mike fought his extradition from Colorado, going even so far as to appeal to the Supreme Court of Colorado. His argument included such legal haystack needles as an erroneous statement at his hearing that the police recovered the M-1 rifle from Mike rather than a bar patron. After losing his extradition battle, he returned to Texas in 1981, the same year I transferred to Mountain View and became the only woman in Texas on Death Row.

The Harris County Grand Jury indicted Mike at the same time as me on both counts of capital murder against Bob Skeens and Robert Banks. Whereas the State decided on the murder conviction of Skeens for me, they chose Banks for Mike. I understand this is rather common in cases involving more than one homicide victim. If, by some legal glitch, Mike or I were not convicted of murdering one of the victims, they could then try us on the other one.

With Skelton's encouragement—civic duty to country and justice for the victims—and not by any subpoena, Linda returned from California to Houston to testify against Mike. Her annulment from Mike eliminated any spousal-immunity issues. Further, acting as her attorney, Skelton made sure there would be no future problems with any prosecution against Linda by insisting that the State grant her immunity for her testimony against Mike. The type of immunity that he obtained was not clear regarding a "use" or "transactional" provision, however, and this would become a legal issue in the future. Skelton was present with Linda at Mike's trial and had coached her on her testimony while she stayed with him in Houston at his one-bedroom condominium for seven to ten days.

Just prior to Mike's trial, the prosecution offered to commute my death penalty to life if I would appear in court against him. I told them,

"No, I can't do that. I don't believe in the death penalty, and I can't be responsible for ending another's life."

"But, Ms. Perillo," said a bewildered-looking assistant district attorney, "we are offering you life over your current death sentence."

"No, I just can't be a party to that."

Mike's attorney sent me a note in which Mike thanked me and said that he understood and knew that if I did testify, he would surely die. He also said that Linda Fletcher was here and was going to testify against him. Earlier, however, in a pre-trial, recorded statement, Mike said, "It doesn't bother me to get the death penalty because I have not made much of my life." This statement brought back memories about my burning urge to confess, which I did physically in the Denver jail and spiritually in the Houston jail. I think that sometimes the soul crumbles within from the very weight of its own evil.

Mike's trial in February 1982 lasted about twice as long as mine. In the punishment phase, the prosecution brought up Mike's previous confinement in San Quentin and his membership in the Aryan Brotherhood. If looks could kill, Mike didn't stand a chance for life imprisonment over the death penalty regarding the special punishment question: "Is there a probability that the defendant would commit acts of violence that would constitute a continuing threat to society?" All it would have taken is for one juror to have voted "no." Instead, "Oh, yes," responded all twelve jurors. Hang 'em Texas-high.

I can imagine that even in his Sunday go-to-trial suit, Mike looked sinister, hard, cruel, unrepentant—years of crime, criminal confine-ment, narcotics, and alcohol had melted moving flesh into expression-less iron. Contrary to the "fair and impartial judgment" ideal, I know from my trial that looks play a big part in the outcome; otherwise, why would the state not have you handcuffed in court wearing a monotone-colored jumpsuit and dragging a ball and chain? Mike, with a micron's chance, might have gotten life were it not for Linda Fletcher's testimony and the fact that the defense made no Penry claims. Penry claims were not available at that time, although Mike did bring them up on appeal.

Johnny Paul Penry[47] was a cause célèbre for opponents to the execution of the mentally "retarded." His case and subsequent U.S. Supreme Court decisions have become a new-millennium crossroad toward execution mercy. Penry was convicted of the rape and murder of Pamela Moseley in Livingston, Texas. Pamela Moseley was the sister of Mark Moseley, a famous NFL football place-kicker. At Penry's trial in mid-1980, a psychologist testified that Penry had the mental age of a six-and-a-half-year-old boy and poor impulse control. In and for the compassionate State of Texas, the jury ignored the defense's plea for mercy based on mitigating circumstances and answered all three special issue questions in the affirmative, and thus rendered the death penalty instead of a life sentence.

Penry appealed twice to the U.S. Supreme Court, which twice reversed his sentence. Texas subsequently retried his case twice more, and twice more gave him the death penalty. In all three trials, Penry received the death penalty. Then the U.S. Supreme Court decided that execution of the mentally retarded should be interpreted as "cruel and unusual punishment" and was not sanctioned by the Eighth Amendment. The State of Texas finally capitulated, and Penry accepted life without parole in 2008 with his stipulation that his plea agreement state that he is not, nor ever was, a person with mental retardation. According to multiple news sources, Johnny Paul Penry still believes in Santa Claus.

Of interest and consideration in Mike Briddle's case is the phrase "mitigating circumstances" as used in the U.S. Supreme Court's reversals of Penry's death penalty regarding his diminished mental capacity. From these decisions, "mitigating circumstances" appears to have evolved into a broader scope that includes trends toward childhood abuse and temporary, drug-induced psychosis. Another instance of a mitigating circumstance that precludes the death penalty has been inferred for eons prior to Penry: vehicular homicide for DWI (driving while intoxicated).

Mike introduced certain mitigating circumstances in his final appeal years later, in 1995. From the court record, Mike's Penry claims included:

his mental and narcotic-induced state during the murder, and

an abnormal childhood void of the usual controls for an "aggressive or impulsive behavior."

Also detailed in the appeal were other mitigating circumstances from the affidavits of friends and family:

Mike was a poor student with dyslexia;

from twelve years of age, Mike went through the revolving doors of various California state institutions where he was medicated with heavy-duty psychotropic drugs such as Thorazine and Prolixin;

Mike suffered a traumatic experience when he was sixteen from a wreck on his motorcycle when it collided with a train. His friend and passenger lost both arms and a leg;

Mike's mother was in an automobile accident when she was pregnant with him, and his birth was four to six weeks late, requiring the extensive use of forceps; and

his psychoanalysis showed borderline personality disorder and the possibility of minimal brain injury.

Mike previously had given his account on some of these points. Most notable was his different version of the motorcycle accident. He stated that he had an assault charge at age seventeen for pushing another youth under a train, causing the youth to lose both arms and a leg. Mike's Penry claims were disallowed because capital defendants cannot base a Penry claim on evidence that might have been but was not actually brought up during trial. Also, appellate courts generally take a use-it-or-lose-it approach to certain points not raised in the original trial. If you didn't bring it up then, sorry, no do-overs—tough luck.

* * *

For a year, I sat alone in the Mountain View Unit, the only woman on Death Row. It was hot with no air-conditioning. Looking at a map of Texas, Gatesville is located a little east of the state's center, the spot where one might think the sun burned hottest, but Gatesville can be a mild 104 degrees compared to other parts of this flame-broiled piece of the United States. With little to do except reflect on a horrible past and think about a minimal future, I suffered. Especially, I suffered spiritually, not just from my inability to speak in tongues but from not accepting that God could be able to forgive me. But thanks be to the Holy Spirit who kept me going, reading Scripture, learning, attending services, and receiving comfort even as I suffered.

From my annual, state-scheduled Pap smear, I discovered that I had developed uterine cancer. They froze five spots *in situ*, and I thought I was cured. During this time, my original trial attorney, William W. Burge, received a ruling from his appeal against the State of Texas, *en banc*. The sole issue in the appeal was my angel in disguise, John O. Vennard, the potential juror who was excluded, challenged for cause, and not permitted by the presiding judge to be questioned by the defense. I remember Mr. Burge being visibly upset at the trial during the dismissal of Vennard. The appeals court determined Vennard to be a "vacillating juror." From the appeal (*Perillo v. State*, No. 68872, Appendix B): "In this instance, a clear reading of Vennard's examination by the prosecuting attorney and the trial judge does not reflect such a firm and fixed attitude and position that would have prevented him from reaching or making an impartial decision as to the appellant's guilt, or deciding the submitted statutory special issues fairly." Death penalty questions were "statutory special issues."

These fifty-plus words of complicated legalese translate into layman's terms in the closing statement of the appeal: "The judgment of the trial court is reversed and the cause remanded." Hallelujah. I would get a new trial. I just *knew* this time that they weren't going to kill me. The reversal occurred in June 1983, and shortly after that, I transferred to the Harris County Jail, which was a new jail. As is often said, "Thank goodness for small favors." The previous facility must have sunk into the ground from the weight of its own filth.

I met another young girl in the tank, and we became good friends. Her lawyer was able to "get her off," and she left to stay with him and his wife, Christina. I called her frequently, and when she wasn't there, Christina accepted the toll call and we would talk. One day Christina asked if she could come see me. "Certainly," I replied, and from that point on, we became very close.

During the pre-trial hearings, motions, etc., I became deathly ill. The cancer had returned. The court postponed the trial while I bounced from hospital to hospital for biopsies and tests. My weight dropped from its normal 115 pounds to eighty-six. Finally, I suppose someone decided that if I died, the courts would lose all their pre-trial expenses, and therefore they entered me into Ben Taub Hospital for a hysterectomy. During my recuperation, Christina brought me a gown, robe, and slippers along with a care package of magazines and treats. Christina was an angel, a saint who came into my life at a divine moment.

After I was able to move around, the legal process moved forward once again. In a *déjà vu* scene in the Harris County Criminal Justice Center, 248th District Criminal Court, the judge appointed me a trial attorney. The judge's name was Woody R. Densen. At first I thought "Woody" was just another proper Texas cowboy name, but I learned later that it was a good-ol'-boy nickname for Woodrow.

My appointed attorney was Mr. Robert O.W. Pelton. Robert Pelton had interned in the Harris County District Attorney's Office prior to graduation from the South Texas College of Law. He also had interned in the law office of Jim Skelton, the same Jim Skelton who represented Linda Briddle at her trial and was with her under her new name, Linda Fletcher, during her testimony against Mike Briddle. Although Pelton had vast experience in other legal areas, he had never tried a capital murder case. He was still associated with Jim Skelton, not so much in a legal sense but as a co-owner of several machine shops.

In an early interview, Pelton told me that his partner, Jim Skelton, was familiar with my case and that he was very interested in helping me, and that he didn't believe I deserved the death penalty. Further, he said Skelton knew the case inside and out because he had defended Linda, and that he felt we both got a raw deal because of our relationship with Mike Briddle. "Would you be willing to talk to him?" Pelton asked. I readily answered in the affirmative, and a short time later, Jim Skelton offered his services and asked me for permission to request the court to appoint him as the lead attorney. I immediately agreed to his offer; however, he did not divulge the fact that during Linda's trial, he portrayed both Mike and me as homicidal monsters.

I thought at that time that it was rather strange that Judge Densen had appointed only one trial attorney for me since I knew from "jailhouse law" that in capital murder cases the defendant always receives two attorneys. Perhaps there had been something behind the scenes where the court wanted me to approve Jim Skelton as the lead attorney, and I was so naïve that I readily did so. I don't think that Robert Pelton—at that point—felt that there could be a conflict of interest in appointing Jim Skelton to my case.

Sometime later, I learned that just several months before my trial and separate from it, the "Hanging DA," John B. Holmes, had filed a writ of mandamus against the presiding judge, Woody Densen. A writ of mandamus (in this case) was a legal instrument brought before a higher court to force a lower court to vacate certain decisions felt questionable under existing statutes. In such cases, it is comparable to "I'm gonna tell my daddy on you." It's an action that the legal profession prefers to avoid because it pits judges and attorneys against each other. In this particular case, filed June 27, 1984, Holmes asked the Texas Court of Criminal Appeals to vacate two pre-trial orders entered by Judge Woody Densen. Holmes was prosecuting a drug-related case against six defendants. Judge Densen not only dismissed the case, he dismissed the case with prejudice, meaning the state could not bring it to trial again. Holmes lost the first complaint regarding dismissal but prevailed against the second in which Judge Densen had granted the defendants immunity from further prosecution. However, the most interesting point regarding this writ was the attorneys who represented Judge Densen: Pelton and Skelton. Yes, the same pair chosen to represent me. Not unusual, as I understand it, as judges often have a group of buddies they select as attorneys for the indigent. That is the how the court-appointed attorney system works.

Also of interest, Judge Densen, in 2010, was indicted on a rather bizarre criminal mischief charge. He was convicted and fined $1,500 for keying his neighbor's car, an event captured on videotape. He did not appeal and publicly and profusely apologized. The State Commission on Judicial Conduct subsequently issued him a public warning.

* * *

As I awaited my trial date in a cell on the third floor of the Harris County Jail, an officer asked me if I would be willing to go upstairs and talk to a young lady for whom the state was seeking the death penalty. This same Harris County DA, John B. Holmes, that sought my execution was riding hard and fast after her—a death posse. When I approached her cell, she introduced herself as Karla Faye Tucker. If the eyes are the mirror of the soul, Karla Faye had none, no more soul than that of a caged animal. She had naturally dark-olive skin, black-olive eyes and tar-black, wavy hair. Even in the bright lights outside her cell, her possibly attractive coloring had taken on a coal-gray pallor and a darkness that amplified her three-inch-deep eye sockets—empty holes from which peered eyes so dull that it was like looking into a skull at midnight. Her flesh clung tightly about a skeleton that I just knew had found its feeble nourishment from whatever few calories drugs possess.

Poor Karla Faye, she had obviously waded through some of the same sewers I had. I wondered if I had looked that horrible when I first entered prison. As the weeks passed, we talked frequently. We had a lot in common: dysfunctional families, siblings, middle-class upbringing, and early drug abuse. We became quite close.

CHAPTER 11

Eventually, I moved from the third to the fourth floor of the county jail. Harris County reserved this floor for high-profile capital cases such as Karla Faye Tucker's and mine. When I was young and at home, I noticed that my classmates mostly ran with those of their same age. As a person matures, I understand the line of age difference blurs and people have friends of all ages. Although back then I wanted to run with those older than I because it gave me a sense of importance, I found that age difference is not much of a consideration between drug users and prison inmates. Although Karla Faye was four years younger, it didn't register when I met her. Besides, at that point she looked much, much older than her years might indicate.

Karla Faye Tucker[48, 49] was born and raised in Houston. She was the third of four sisters whose first names also began with the letter K. Her father, a longshoreman, was absent from home for long periods. Her mother, Carolyn Tucker, appeared to be the typical nice little house-wife. Karla Faye was a natural athlete, thin and muscular with innate coordination. At a family-owned lakefront house on Caney Creek near Brazoria, Texas, about an hour from their home in Houston, she devel-oped more of her natural athletic skills, swimming and diving. The diving got her into trouble in later years when she dove off a cliff in Austin and dislocated her shoulder.

Although unverified, this was probably Hamilton Pool[50] in Dripping Springs, just outside of Austin. Against the park rules, many a brave soul sneaks up on the cliff and jumps feetfirst. Only Karla Faye would have had the nerve to dive headfirst instead.

Karla Faye terminated her childhood when she started smoking mari-juana at age eight and was into drugs and sex by age twelve. At age fourteen, she dropped out of school and traveled with her mother, a rock groupie, following the Allman Brothers Band, the Marshall Tucker

Band, and the Eagles. In step with her mother's example, prostitution in return for drugs became a way of life.

She had always wondered why she looked different from her sisters, and sometime during her teens, she vocally questioned the fact that she was dark—dark skin, black hair, and black eyes—while the rest of the family was light with fair skin, blonde hair, and blue eyes. When, through persistence, she learned she was the product of an extramarital affair, and her father whom she loved dearly was not her real father, her self-esteem plummeted. Upon her mother's death, when Karla Faye turned twenty, she grieved heavily and found comfort by digging even deeper into the mud that life can offer.

She tried marriage while continuing to engage in prostitution even with her husband's knowledge, but she decided she needed still more freedom, like the freedom to run with an element whose very actions symbolize an independent lifestyle. She wanted the identity of a biker. Through friends, she met Danny Garrett, a biker and part-time bartender. They enjoyed a drug-house communal life in Spring Branch, a suburb of Houston. Friends came and went, slept, did drugs, and worshiped the Harley-Davidson, the American-made supreme deity of motorcycles.

Jerry Dean was one of the frequent bikers who visited their house, a person to whom Karla Faye took a deep, personal hatred, with almost a demonic rage—he just wasn't tough enough to be a biker, and he didn't deserve to own a Harley.

One night in June 1983, at 3 a.m., Karla Faye, Danny, and another friend, after doing a considerable quantity of drugs, broke into Dean's apartment with the sole purpose of stealing the parts and frame to a Harley that Dean was rebuilding. Murdering Dean was never mentioned prior to their intrusion. In a landlord's nightmare, Dean kept all of his tools strewn about the inside of his apartment—tools in every room, including the bedroom, and the Harley in the living room, with oil dripping down along the kickstand and puddling on the carpet.

After Karla Faye and Danny entered Dean's apartment, they went into the bedroom where Karla Faye sat on the unsuspecting Dean as Danny drove a hammer that he found on the floor into the back of Dean's skull several times. This action broke Dean's neck and his head flopped over and entrapped his last gasps as a gurgle through a blood-blocked windpipe. Karla Faye yelled, "Stop making those noises," and grabbed a nearby pickaxe with which she struck him several times. Danny, who had left to carry out the motorcycle frame, returned to the bedroom and gave Dean the final *coup de grâce*.

After Danny had left the room to load more motorcycle parts into his truck, Karla Faye noticed a woman hiding under the covers on the bed. Deborah Thornton, a girl Dean had picked up at a party the afternoon before, was in the proverbial wrong place at the wrong time. Karla Faye went after her with the pickaxe, and after several blows, Danny returned and embedded the ax in her throat. If not for a shoulder weakened from dislocation in her diving accident, Karla Faye might have rendered the final blow in both instances. At Karla Faye's trial, several of her "friends" testified that she later told them that she experienced multiple orgasms while swinging the pickaxe on both victims.

When we first met, she almost seemed willing to accept death as her punishment. Talking to her about God and forgiveness through Jesus Christ brought nothing but blank looks from unfeeling eyes. I hate to use the term "stone-faced," because everyone tosses it about so often, but there was no emotion in her expressions.

Karla Faye Tucker mugshot[51]

"What I wanted to be, and where I was headed, was a professional hit-woman," she said, and she said it so mechanically.

I know Karla Faye would be the first to admit that she was "codependent." She needed someone, ideally a man, to make decisions for her. When it wasn't a man, it was her mother. As we talked more, I learned that her dream before she got into drugs was to be a gymnast. She was so limber and could do the splits with such ease. I've seen her jump from a sitting position on a bench and hold her arms and legs straight out in midair.

Karla Faye, however, did not complete her trial as the same person who entered the Harris County Jail. Watching a spiritually based puppet show performed by a group from Teen Challenge, she became curious and took one of the Bibles they had placed on a table.

Later she recalled, "I didn't know what I was reading. Before I knew it, I was in the middle of my cell, on the floor and on my knees. I was just asking God to forgive me."

When I saw Karla Faye after this, she was a new person. No longer was she like an emaciated black alley cat on the prowl, an animal wary of all around her. Her eyes sparkled, and you could look into them and see a new creature. Even her dull black hair had taken on luster. We laughed. We cried. We prayed. We began our long-lost childhoods together as new babies in Christ. Karla Faye had no reservations, no qualms, and no doubts that God had forgiven her through Christ Jesus. Her conversion was such a blessing to me and helped to ease my spiritual uncertainties and reassure me of my salvation.

Praying with Karla Faye, I noticed how natural it is to pray for others and not to pray for yourself. I know that the prayers of others protect us. We prayed fervently during the punishment phase of her trial, and God answered our prayers, as He always does—not as we had hoped, but saying that He had other plans for Karla Faye Tucker. The jury gave her death by lethal injection. I don't know why at least one of the twelve couldn't see the shiny new penny before them, that she had "put off the old man and his deeds and have put on the new man,"[52] and that she was "in Christ, a new creature: old things are passed away."[53]

By 1984, the State of Texas had changed the mandatory-affirmative, special issue questions before the jury to render the death penalty. They reduced them from three to two but retained the most important one in both our cases:

> "Whether there is a probability that the defendant would commit criminal acts of violence that would constitute a continuing threat to society."

Why could no one see there was no probability, no possibility of this whatsoever? Perhaps God hardened their hearts like He did Pharaoh's; certainly He had planned a glorious exodus for Karla Faye. When she returned to the fourth-floor tank, we cried and prayed together. She repeatedly prayed for me not to receive the same verdict in my trial, and I prayed for her to receive a miracle like I had, a successful appeal granting a new trial. Most of all, we prayed for the families of our victims: for their peace and for their forgiveness.

Karla Faye Tucker is the subject of many books, a movie, and even several songs. The two books I have read are *Crossed Over*[54] and *Karla Faye Tucker Set Free*.[55] The first one is more of a true-crime novel that details the homicides. The second, the one I like better, details her spiritual conversion and the fantastic creature that evolved—a newborn butterfly, full of life and never at rest.

After Karla Faye's trial, the state kept her there in order to testify against her fall partner, Danny Garrett. It was very difficult for her because she truly loved Danny.

"I feel so bad about this, Pam. If I testify, I know Danny will get the death penalty for sure. I just wonder if I should do this. I know God is telling me to come completely clean, but I just don't know."

"God has spoken to your heart," I told her. "You know that He wants you to tell the truth. I did not testify against my fall partner because I didn't feel it right in my heart, but you know He wants you to testify."

"But then I would be a snitch. I shouldn't do this to him, but I feel inside that I must."

"Karla, trust in God. He's leading you."

We talked a lot about this and prayed that God would give her strength. Having to see Danny every day in court was hard on her, but after it was over, he wrote and told her that he understood and still loved her. During this period, we frequently sat in the same waiting area of the criminal justice center; she was there to testify at Danny's trial, and I at my own trial.

* * *

"Pam," Karla Faye asked, "you remember my execution number, the one they gave me on my mugshot when I entered?"

"I sure do. It was 777. You mumbled something back when we first met about it being good luck and gave a fake 'ha-ha.' You know different now, right?"

"Yes, it's a Godly number. The number seven appears more than any other number in the Bible, and God gave me three of them. I am so blessed, so blessed to have lived long enough to accept my Savior, Christ Jesus," and two pairs of eyes glistened.

Years later, I had the Christian fish, three crosses, and the number 777 tattooed behind my ear.

"Did I tell you about the execution number on my mugshot?" I asked. "It was 665. I missed the mark of the beast by one number. I have often wondered about the next person, the one who got 666."

Danny, of course, did get the death sentence, and Karla Faye transferred to Mountain View Death Row. My trial continued for another four months. Back then, inmates could write to each other; now they cannot. We wrote to each other often. She said she was so lonely, being the only one on Death Row at Mountain View, having no contact with anyone. Gosh, could I sympathize with her.

CHAPTER 12

During the preliminaries for my new trial, Christina and her husband, along with Jim Skelton and Robert Pelton, flew to California to visit with my family. Christina is the woman I had become friends with before I became ill at the start of the second trial. They arranged a flight back—Christina paid for it—for my older sister, Joanne; my dad; my stepmom, Helen; my half-sister, Donna (daughter of my dad and Helen); and my son, Joseph. While they were there, Christina asked Joseph whether my dad and Helen were his parents.

He responded, "Oh, no. They're not my mom and daddy. I have a mom, and someday she is going to come and get me."

Christina and her husband graciously allowed them to stay in their home during the trial. I had not seen my son since he was a year and a half old. He was now six. My dad and stepmom never wrote me—so frustrating and painful, not knowing anything about my son. When Joseph walked into the courtroom, I noticed he had a severe limp. When I questioned Dad and Helen about it, Helen said, "Why, he has always limped like that." It made me feel so inept, so depressed.

On October 8, 1984, in the same 248th District courtroom as my first trial but now with Judge Woodrow (Woody) Densen presiding, my trial started in the usual manner with the game of *voir dire*. This Old French term literally means "to speak the truth" and was intended, through a series of questions, to weed out viable jurors from those who might not be able to render a fair verdict because of such issues as racial bias, preconceived notions, kinship, etc. Now it has become, in addition to its original intent, a head game in which the opposing lawyers wrangle to select the jurors they feel will be more likely to vote for their side. Through a thorny field of rules, the attorneys from each side step lightly with questions for prospective jurors and hope they don't accidentally crush the fragile roots of a no-no plant that would eventually necessitate a retrial.

Each side has a certain number of peremptory strikes (somewhere around ten in number, depending on the criminal district in which the trial occurs). A peremptory strike means the attorney can tell the juror, "We don't want you. Goodbye," without giving any reason for the dismissal. Oh, but beware if the juror is or is not the same color or gender as the defendant depending on the side who strikes, for therein lies bias danger: grounds for an appeal. Each side also has an unlimited number of strikes for cause, a point that was particularly important in my first trial. If a potential juror is not *death qualified*, i.e. he openly states that he would not be able to render the death penalty, then after questioning by the defense and the judge, it's basically, "Mr. Wuss, you are excused. Thank you for your time."

The reason I was able to get a second trial was, of course, due to a vacillating venireman, Mr. John O. Vennard, in my first trial. There was another vacillating venireman in this trial, Mrs. Griggs. Mrs. Griggs do-si-doed (as they say in Texas square dancing) around being able to render the death penalty or not, and the prosecution, of course, challenged her for cause. Judge Densen obviously did not want a repeat of Vennard, so he questioned her and then gave her time to think it over during a long lunch recess. When she returned, she unequivocally stated that she would not support the death penalty. Judge Densen then wisely allowed the defense to question Mrs. Griggs, an act disallowed in my first trial for venireman Vennard. After being satisfied with her response, Judge Densen said, "Mrs. Griggs, you are excused. Thank you for your time."

The game is somewhat like the childhood card game Go Fish. Each player gets so many cards and tries to guess what his opponent has and will play.

"I'll sacrifice this Catholic card that most probably doesn't believe in the

death penalty because there are some better ones still in the deck, and I might get your Baptist card that most probably believes in the death penalty."

"No," says the defense, "you cannot have my gray-haired, makeup-free, old-lady hippie. Go Fish."

The game goes on for days until the court selects twelve jurors and a few alternates. Jury selection is so recognized as a game that I understand one can now play it on the Internet.[56] In an Internet game, a player is given a hypothetical case and the choice of prosecution or defense. He looks at a selection of potential jurors, their religions, professions, etc., and chooses the one he thinks best for his position. After selecting all the jurors he is allowed (six or twelve), a point system determines how well he performed. They should rename jury selection from *voir dire* to what it truly is, a head game, then translate it into some fancy foreign phrase, or better yet, still in French, *jeu de tête*. My lawyers felt that we won the head game with a rather good selection. Even the assistant district attorney, Sid Crowley, told me I probably would not get the death penalty.

Several days before *jeu de tête* in my trial, Mike Briddle and another Death Row inmate at the Ellis I Unit outside Huntsville constructed a crude fire bomb and tossed it into the cell of a black man, Calvin J. Williams, all in the name of racism and the ideals of Mike's Aryan Brotherhood. The fact that Calvin's murder victim was a white woman might have intensified the Brotherhood's punishment. The *Houston Chronicle*—following the media's mantra, *if it bleeds it leads*—splashed my name in the paper and a recount of my crime along with Mike's former prison record and membership in the Brotherhood. I got his guilt by association. Just what I needed to influence my upcoming jury! Williams, the black inmate, was severely burned, and his fate never fared for the better after that. In 1990, another Death Row inmate strangled him to death with a jump rope in the recreation yard at the Ellis I Unit.

I have since learned that the next mugshot number from the State of Texas following my 665, the number 666, the mark of the beast, was assigned to Calvin J. Williams.[57] Although not one to believe in hexes or numerology, I still feel that the coincidence was eerie.

During these early proceedings, Christina's husband arranged lunches with my family and me in an anteroom to the court during recess. Judge Woody Densen approved. Below is a picture of my son, Joseph, and me taken by my dad during one of these gatherings. Christina gave me the dress I am wearing. She brought me a new dress every day for the trial.

Pamela and Joseph, second trial, 1984

Formal testimony began November 5, and where was my lead attorney, Jim Skelton? Jim Skelton's absence at the opening of my trial was disturbing, to say the least. The trial started as somewhat of a mirror image of my first trial. The prosecution read my first confession, the written one taken in Denver, word for word. Then Officer West took the stand to recount my second confession. This was the verbal one given on the plane returning from Denver when I said that Linda and Mike were not involved, and I had killed both Banks and Skeens by myself. Officer West made a simple and brief statement of his testimony, the same as he had given in my first trial. No surprises thus far.

I continued through the trial feeling I had a relatively good chance of not getting the death penalty; that is, until Linda Briddle, now Linda

Fletcher, took the stand for the prosecution. Unbeknownst to me at the time, Judge Densen had issued a subpoena to Linda during *voir dire* on October 19, compelling her to return to Texas to testify for the state. She had called Skelton to help her fight the subpoena through the California courts, and that was where he was on the first day of my trial. On this point, Skelton was representing me, as it was not in my best interest for Linda to testify against me, and initially, his being there with her was to my advantage. Skelton surely knew this, but some strange events took place in California, events that I am now sure were God-ordained.

The appellate record, Case 94-20759, Appendix B, states, "The period of time when Skelton was in California is a black hole; we have no information about what happened at the hearing." What did happen, however, was that the State of Texas formally offered Linda transactual immunity in return for her testimony against me. The issue between "use" and "transactual immunity" came up in Linda's testimony at Mike Briddle's trial. With formal transactual immunity, she could never be tried in Texas in the future for the murder of Skeens or Banks, a King's X card, but she had to uphold her part, namely to testify against me. Skelton now had a readily apparent conflict of interest: representing Fletcher against me. She and he both returned to Houston a day or so after my trial began. Again unbeknownst to me but noted in an appellate record, Linda initially stayed at a hotel arranged for by the state, but shortly thereafter, she moved into Skelton's condominium for the rest of my trial.

"Ms. Fletcher," asked the bailiff, "do you swear to tell the truth and nothing but the truth, so help you God?" I was naïve enough then to think she would.

"Were you present during the murder of Robert Skeens?" asked the prosecution.

"No," she responded and stared straight at the back of the courtroom.

She never looked at me except one time to identify me according to the court's request.

"Were you present during the murder of Bob Banks?" Again, "No."

I kicked Jim Skelton under the table and whispered, "She's lying. Ask her about the blood on her blue jeans that they found in Denver. Ask her about *her* bloody fingerprint on one of the victim's glasses."

"There, there," said Skelton as he patted my hand. "Don't worry. Everything's going to be okay."

But it wasn't. Every chance she could, Linda answered the prosecution's questions in a manner that made me out to be a monster, and Skelton sat there like a concrete garden statue. He never once objected to anything from the prosecution's questioning. I now had the sickening feeling that I had been set up. When it became the defense's turn to cross-examine Linda, I was one hundred percent convinced of a setup. Skelton began his questions by detailing his personal and professional relationship with Fletcher, and how he had met with her and the victims' families in order to elicit her testimony at Mike Briddle's trial.

"What?" I mouthed. She had talked to the families?

I had begged Skelton to let me talk to them and say with every part of my heart and soul how I was sorry for what had happened. But no, he wouldn't let me. But he let her?

Skelton also brought up her "silver spoon" background and education. *What a precious, misguided little girl. Why, she couldn't possibly be lying.* Next, he asked her about what had happened, essentially a repetition of what she had already told the prosecution previously about the Perillo Monster, and he never questioned anything. Then he asked her about points not brought up by the prosecution where she could testify to my "heavy drug involvement," and that I helped Briddle with his "robberies." About the drugs, I couldn't argue; they were responsible for the mess I was in. But *robberies* with Mike and noted in the plural? There was only one with Mike, and again, no questioning or clarification on Skelton's part.

It was later noted that Skelton had discussed the questions for his cross-examination with Linda earlier, and that he did not want her to slip up and contradict anything from her testimony against Briddle. According to the appellate record, "Skelton led Fletcher through her testimony so consistently that the transcript reads as though Skelton himself is testifying. Throughout the lengthy cross-examination, Fletcher predominately gave one-word responses to lengthy, compound questions posed by Skelton."

Obvious to me and thankfully to others, Skelton had a conflict of interest. During a recess, I approached Judge Woody Densen at the bench.

"Judge Densen, I just have to say this. I feel that Jim Skelton is not asking Linda Fletcher the right questions when I know that she is lying. I feel—I know—that he has a conflict of interest."

"Ms. Perillo, we will deal with that if it arises."

The guilty verdict came swiftly. I expected as much. The punishment phase was the crucial issue, and I knew as I prayed for God's mercy in their verdict that I would soon join Karla Faye on Death Row. In this part of the trial, Skelton recalled Officer West to the stand—a rather bizarre move, I thought. *Why bring my reckless, singular confession out again in the punishment phase?* After a few cursory questions, Skelton asked, "Officer West, what did you say when Ms. Perillo said that she killed both Banks and Skeens by herself?"

"I asked how could someone as small as she do that all by herself?"

"And she replied?"

"She said, 'Give me a rope and a gun and I'll show you,'" and the Perillo Monster grew larger and uglier.

At the end of the day, I once again begged my attorneys, Skelton and Pelton, to let me testify on my own behalf.

"I can explain all of that behind the second confession. I wanted Mike and Linda to get away while I was in jail. I was so young—the rope-and-gun statement was just a flippant remark. And I want to set the record straight about Linda's testimony. She's lying. She wouldn't know the truth if it smacked her upside the head."

"No," they chorused, "if you testify, they'll dig into your past and make you look even worse."

"Worse? I'm not a bad person. Other than being a child runaway and involved in drugs and a robbery, I never did anything really bad before this," I said, but they would not yield.

My sister, Joanne, testified on my behalf. My dad, stepmother, half-sister, and son already had returned to California after the jury selection. Since my dad said he couldn't handle it anymore, we all agreed they should leave.

I couldn't have known that would be the last time I would see my father. He died in 1987. None of my family contacted me. I found out about his death sixteen days after he had passed, from Christina.

Joseph and Pamela's father, circa 1984

Warden Plane[58] from Mountain View, a witness for the state to testify against me, turned it around by saying that I was a Christian convert and a model prisoner.

Then the state brought up the fact that I had been written up at

Mountain View for a flagrant violation of the rules. They never disclosed the "heinous" details of this crime: I had held back two small boxes of cereal from my breakfast tray to eat later. "If Ms. Perillo can't follow the rules in a state institution, how could she follow the rules in society?" And Skelton sat there with his face etched in cement.

The prosecution introduced the details of my robbery with Mike Briddle and the still-outstanding warrant from California. The robbery victim had since passed away, or I am sure the state would have treated him to another Houston vacation in return for his testimony. Members from both the victims' families, the Skeenses and the Bankses, testified. Prior to their testimony, Jim Skelton told me that he planned to interview the Skeens family. I begged him to let me talk to them. I wanted so badly to say I was sorry and ask for their forgiveness, but he wouldn't allow it. I never heard what transpired in that interview. On November 14, my attorneys and I rose for the punishment verdict.

"Mr. Foreman, has the jury reached a verdict?" asked Judge Densen.

"We have, your honor."

"And how do you answer for the first special question: whether there is a probability that the defendant would commit criminal acts of violence that would constitute a continuing threat to society."

"We unanimously answer in the affirmative."

"And the second question regarding mitigating circumstances for a life sentence instead of the death penalty?"

"We unanimously answered in the negative."

After the noise in the courtroom subsided, Judge Densen pronounced the sentence: death by lethal injection. As the words fell, Robert Pelton and I embraced and cried together.

CHAPTER 13

Not all good comes free of the bad, and not all bad comes free of the good. A miracle did take place before the bad part of my trial. Christina and her husband asked me if I would like them to bring Joseph to Texas to live in their home. After I readily responded, "Yes," we asked Joseph the same question as we all gathered in the visiting room. I will never forget his reply, "You don't want to miss me anymore, do you, Mom?" Then he turned to Christina, "I knew I had a momma, and I've been waiting for her to come get me."

Joseph returned with the rest of the family before formal testimony, but when he came back to Texas, through the action of the courts, I now had another mom. I had two before then: my biological mom, Wuanita, long passed away, and my stepmom, Helen. My third mom, Christina, is my adopted mom. She and her husband legally adopted me so they could raise Joseph as their grandson. Joseph would still be my son and would be living in Texas near me. I thought my heart would burst with joy.

My dad and Helen were not happy with this new arrangement. I can understand, because Joseph was a sweet and loveable child. But he was my son, and it was my decision. I knew he would have a better life in Texas than with them. My insight was correct; Joseph has grown into a straight and righteous Christian man.

Joseph's new grandparents, Christina and her husband, arranged a medical correction for his limp. They sent him to the best of private schools, then to Baylor University, and finally to Texas A&M, from which he received his college degree. Joseph is one hundred percent "straight arrow," as they say in Texas. He doesn't smoke or drink, is married with a family, and best of all, he is a good Christian man. My spirit quivers when I think about what might have happened to him if it hadn't been for Christina. Christina is the God-woven, golden thread that borders the tapestry of my life.

"My life is just a weaving," a tapestry woven by God, as taken from the poem "The Weaver."[59]

The Weaver, Verse I

My life is just a weaving
Between my Lord and me.
I cannot change the color
For He works most steadily.

My blanket started out as a dog's blanket—dirty, frayed, and full of ticks and fleas—but now that I am redeemed, it has been made new and made whole. I wrote this poem for Christina one Mother's Day.

Christina

A Mother's Day Poem
Pamela Perillo

I praise you on this Mother's Day
For all that you have done
Choosing me and Joseph
We knew you were the one
Mothers usually shop for kids
With smiles all aglow
Christina went against the grain
And took one from Death Row
Joseph only six years old
Not knowing what was wrong
Your loving arms around him
He knew where he belonged

You raised him up and on your own
Today an Aggie man
He's all grown-up and happy
This was Christina's plan
Today, years have passed
Two trials gone astray
Now we face another one
And by my side you stay
You said where you come from
Mothers never go away
You always proved your love for me
In a very special way
I think when God made you
With love as pure as light
Sent you to me with hopes and dreams
To help me win this fight

After my trial, I tried hard to get some badly needed dental work performed in Houston. Mike Barber tried to get a court stay, so I could get this done, but the judge thought otherwise. Mike Barber was a prominent NFL football player who retired early to minister to prison inmates through Mike Barber Ministries.[60] I learned a lot from him, and he has been a help and a blessing to me all these years.

When I arrived back at Mountain View in Gatesville, Karla Faye and I had a long, bittersweet reunion with many tears. She was so glad to see me and yet so sad to hear about my sentence. Her cell was across from mine and we could talk at will. My cell looked out on the rec yard, whereas Karla Faye's looked out on the parking area. She said she could see three crosses (actually telephone poles) and knew which one was hers—"next to the one in the middle, the Penitent Thief who will see paradise."

As noted earlier, Death Row was at the end of a hall housing cells for Ad Seg, and we were also close to the cells reserved for psych patients. Often one of the girls in Psych would tie her sheet to the door to impede entry, spread flammable bedding, paper, etc., in the middle of her cell, and start a fire—inmates could smoke then and had matches. Karla Faye and I, of course, could not leave our cells and had to lie on the floor with a blanket over our head to keep from coughing up our innards. For extra spite came the usual excrement tossing at the guards on some sort of prearranged signal. Their mess always seemed to land in front of our cells. One of our neighboring Ad Seg and Psych inmate's favorite diversions was the blanket party. Again, on some unknown signal, they would stuff their blankets down their commodes and flush repeatedly until water ran ankle-deep everywhere. We were constantly dry-docking our belongings from the floor during one of their high-tide parties.

And was it ever hot! Texas summers never relented except *sort of* in the early morning—sometimes. In the morning, if the temperature was exceedingly warm, expect a noonday scorcher. If the day began unbearably hot and muggy, expect the afternoon to be boiled up from the center of the earth.

It was still lava-hot time when my distinction of being the oldest female on Death Row ended. In the fall of 1985, Betty Lou Beets came to Mountain View. Betty Lou Beets was forty-eight years of age when she joined Karla Faye and me. She was pretty, with bleached hair and a good figure, but she was bitter and obviously not a Christian. Karla Faye and I knew when we first met her that we had a divinely prepared mission before us.

Betty Lou Beets (née Dunevant) was born in North Carolina from, as they say, "humble beginnings," in a cabin without water and electricity. Measles almost killed her at an early age and left her with very little hearing. At age five, she remembers being raped, but she didn't know by whom and didn't understand why she "was hurting and my mother and aunt tried to help me. I remember them trying to put something back into me as if my insides were falling out."[61]

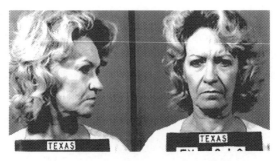

Betty Lou Beets, mugshot, 1985

When Betty Lou was twelve, her mother suffered a mental break-down and was institutionalized for several months, so Betty Lou quit school to help raise her younger brother and sister. Gradually her mother improved, returned home, and resumed working until she retired at age sixty-five. Later in life, Betty Lou learned that mental or physical abuse by a long line of males started with her grandmother and progressed through five generations, past herself and on to her grandchildren.

"Where does it stop and where does it end? I wish it could with me, but it has already gone on ahead of me."[(62)]

She married at fifteen and had six children. Longing for something missing from her teens, she started frequenting bars. Her disgruntled husband of seventeen years filed for divorce. Betty Lou soon married another man who often abused her. Following their divorce and amidst contradictory testimonies, she shot him several times as he entered their back door. After a lengthy stay in the hospital, he dropped all charges and they remarried, a reconciliation that lasted one month.

Soon she found another man at a bar, and they lived together for four years before marriage. That marriage lasted a little more than a year. Betty Lou's next marriage, one of constant fighting, lasted less than her last one. However, her ex begged her to take him back; they remarried and moved to Cedar Creek Lake near Gun Barrel City, located in the transitional geographic region between eastern Texas (Big Thicket and swamps) and central Texas (Hill Country). Betty Lou bought a lot near the lake, and her new fourth husband bought a two-bedroom trailer for their home. This marriage soon culminated in a familiar pattern of physical abuse. After the abuse began, Betty Lou shot her husband as he lay sleeping in their bed. After a long struggle to stuff him into a sleeping bag and drag him into a closet, she called one of her daughters, who agreed to help bury him. They dumped him into a pre-dug hole in the backyard and later covered him with patio stones.

Betty Lou met her final husband, Jimmy Don Beets, while tending bar at the Cedar Club on Texas State Highway 274 about five miles from Gun Barrel City. Jimmy Don was a fire captain in Dallas and made the long commute (fifty-plus miles) from Cedar Creek Lake because of his obsessive enjoyment of boating, drinking, and fishing. Betty Lou became Betty Lou Beets in 1982, and her new husband moved into her trailer, the one her previous husband had purchased before "disappearing." Jimmy Don never abused Betty Lou; she decided to kill him for a $100,000 insurance policy and his fire department retirement benefits. Using the same *modus operandi* for killing her fourth husband, she shot Jimmy Don in bed and this time had her son help bury him in a sleeping bag under a wishing well in the front yard. This repeat performance earned Betty Lou the moniker of the "Black Widow Killer." Killing Jimmy Don for money bought her a capital murder charge and the death penalty.

Betty Lou Beets entered the cell next to me on my right. It was a most fortuitous location, because we didn't look directly at each other, and we bumped heads from the start. I don't know why—maybe just one of those feelings you get when you first meet someone and know you are not going to be friends. She could become hysterical rather easily. Late one warm autumn night, the alarms went off and the lights pulsed. The smell of burning paper wafted through the ventilation system.

"We're on fire!" she screamed. "We're gonna be burned alive!"

"Get down on the floor and cover your head with a blanket!" yelled Karla Faye.

"Help! Save me!"

We heard her muffled cry and intense sobbing for the duration of another one of our Psych bonfires.

From the details of her life history, Betty Lou obviously needed male attention. And if not from a male, then she needed attention as a victim—especially from the media—for being handicapped with a hearing loss or serving as a poster child for the abused wife. But her hearing handicap didn't hamper our conversation because she now had hearing aids, and regardless of whatever sort of love-hate relationship we shared, she always seemed to come to me in a crisis, to cry on my shoulder.

Her I-am-a-victim attitude was clearly expressed when the state turned down one of her appeals. In a screaming rage, she grabbed an 8-by-10 picture of Jimmy Don taped to her wall, shredded it into little pieces, and flung it into the hall. "It's all his fault!" she yelled. She was cold and aloof. It took a long time to get her to warm up to Karla Faye and me, and even then, she still kept her distance. I think she had some events in her early life that caused her never to trust women in general. She always seemed to think another woman was trying to steal her husband.

She did find salvation, but Karla Faye and I felt her relationship with God was not as joyful as it could have been. Whenever there was a crisis in her life, she never would let go and trust God. It was always *poor, poor, pitiful me.* But our desire for her peace and joy was not in judgment, for we all must "work out our own salvation..."[63] and we all shall worship the Savior in our own way.

CHAPTER 14

When the New Year of 1986 arrived under a blanket of wind and cold rain, we three—Karla Faye, Betty Lou, and I—moved to a new Death Row unit—a move we compared to one from hell to heaven. The new Death Row was air-conditioned. When summer came to Texas, words crumble in describing the comparison between with and without air-conditioning. Our new unit had a separate rec yard, day room, work-room, and eight cells (three for us and five empty). Perhaps the elected politicians were expecting a lot more females in their quest to be tough on crime.

In our workroom, we made Parole Pal dolls. These resembled the popular Cabbage Patch Dolls made from yarn and cloth patches. The prison would sell these to the guards and other state employees. Warden Plane, who had testified for me at my second trial, had retired, and we now had Warden Pamela S. Baggett.[64]

* * *

Frances Elaine Newton joined us on Death Row in the fall of 1988. Three weeks prior to her alleged murder of her family outside of Houston (Harris County), Frances purchased an automobile insurance policy. An aggressive salesperson suggested life insurance as well. Frances had recently lost three infant cousins in a house fire, and her relatives did not have enough money to bury them. Frances, because of her recent loss and on the advice of her father, was very amenable to the concept of life insurance and purchased a $50,000 policy on her husband and another on her daughter. This simple, emotionally based act became the motive for a capital murder charge in the execution-style shooting of her husband, Adrian; her daughter, Farrah; and her son, Alton. The state "clearly" had a motive, the first of the three criteria (motive, means, opportunity) for criminal guilt, but could not explain why Frances shot Alton, who had no insurance policy.

On the evening of the murders, Frances left her apartment when all three of her family were still alive and drove a short distance to visit Sondra Nelms, her paternal cousin. Frances and her husband were having severe marital problems, primarily because he was a user and a dealer of narcotics. They were, however, trying to reconcile, a fact that Frances shared with Sondra when she left Sondra's home. Before the two cousins returned to Frances' apartment for a visit, Sondra saw Frances deposit a blue bag in a burned-out, abandoned house next door—the same house where her three infant cousins died, a house that belonged to Frances' father. Frances placed this blue bag while Sondra watched. Sondra did not ask for an explanation, and Frances did not volunteer one. Frances and Sondra returned to Frances' apartment and found Adrian, Farrah, and Alton dead. Frances went into hysterics and appeared visibly shaken.

Later that same evening, Sondra led police to the blue bag that contained a .25 pistol. When questioned, Frances said she found the pistol in their home, and that since her husband, Adrian, had been involved in a drug dispute over $1,500 that he owed his dealer, she didn't want a strange gun in the house. The police later found that this gun belonged to Frances' high school boyfriend with whom she was having an affair. Adrian was having an extra-marital affair of his own.

On the day following the murders, the police examined the gun for a ballistic match and reported it to be the murder weapon. In an unexplained and abnormal delay, the police did not arrest Frances until two weeks later. On that same day following the murders, the police took Frances to her apartment, where she pointed out the clothes she had worn the day before. Immediately, they examined her hands for gunshot residue using an atomic absorption test and found none, but they did find nitrate particles on the lower part of the dress that she had worn. Nitrates occur in gunpowder and also in fertilizer. From the position of the particles, she would have had to have shot her family with her hands on the floor. The nitrates could have been from fertilizer that her twenty-one-month-old daughter, Farrah, touched on the day of the murders. Her daughter might have grabbed the hem of her dress. The state, however, used a destructive test, thus compromising verification of the type of nitrates and, further, stored the dress with other clothing, thereby cross-contaminating it beyond use. For all purposes, the state destroyed exculpatory evidence.

Further lack of evidence in this circumstantial case included no nitrates on any of Frances' other clothes, no blood on any of her clothes, no blood on the pistol, no blood in the sinks or shower in her apartment, and no blood in her car. During the trial, there was mention of another gun identical to that used in the murders, but further elaboration vanished in contradiction and silence. Inexplicably, the fact that a neighbor heard a gunshot at a time when Frances could not have been present never surfaced. "The witnesses all agree that Newton was not at the apartment at [that time]."[65] Also, an unidentified witness called the Harris County Sheriff's Department and said she saw a red pickup truck at the scene driven by a black male she thought to be about thirty years old. The caller gave them a license plate number, but no follow-up action appears to have taken place. Nonetheless, the state now "clearly" had the second criteria for guilt: the means.

The state "clearly" found an opportunity that was even more unrealistic than motive and means. In a twenty-minute period, Frances would have had to kill her family, remove all blood from herself and her clothing, and clean her hands of all gunpowder residue—a physical impossibility within the time period before testing.

The corker to this empty bottle of justice came from two sources: Frances' court-appointed attorney, Mr. Ronald G. Mock, and the prosecution's psychiatrist, Dr. Charles Covert. Two months after the court appointed Mock to be Frances' attorney, Frances knew something was amiss and wrote a letter to the trial judge stating that because of his minimal contact with her, it was like having no attorney at all. A month later, still represented by Mock, who appeared to continue doing nothing, Frances filed a motion to dismiss him and have the court appoint her a new counsel, stating that she had "no faith or confidence" in Mock. Without a hearing, the court denied the motion on the day of its receipt.

The week before the trial started, Frances' family was able to gather enough money to hire a new attorney rather than have Frances' fate rest in Mock's hands. On the day the trial was to begin, the court held a hearing to grant a substitution and a continuance so the new attorney might prepare a viable case. Mock was asked if he had talked to Sondra Nelms, and he replied, "I tell you I'm a lawyer; I'm not an investigator."[66] He was further asked the names of any witnesses (for the prosecution or defense) that he had talked to. He replied that he couldn't do so "off the top of his head."[67] In truth, Mock had not interviewed anyone and had not subpoenaed any witnesses for the defense on the day the trial was to begin. Although the court agreed to the substitution of new counsel, it would not grant the continuance. This act, in effect, kept Mock as Frances' attorney. Because of Mock's lack of investigation, the jury never knew many facts concerning Frances Newton:

1) That the police appeared to have recovered two pistols;

2) That it took two weeks after the ballistics examination before they arrested her;

3) Whether the nitrates on her skirt were from gunpowder or fertilizer;

4) That there was a trail of blood in the apartment, thus amplifying the fact that there was no blood anywhere on Frances' person or in her car;

5) That only a basically impossible, narrow window of twenty minutes existed during which Frances could have killed her family and removed all evidence connecting her to the crime;

6) That a witness noted the time of the crime from the sound of a gunshot when the state's witness placed Frances elsewhere;

7) That a witness saw a red pickup truck at the scene during the crime and took down the license-plate number;

8) That the police did not pursue any investigation of the red pickup truck; and

9) That Frances was emotionally vulnerable to an insurance salesman's pitch when she purchased life insurance on her husband and daughter, and that she purchased none on her son, who also was murdered.

Had these facts come forth, "no reasonable juror would have found her guilty."[68] But they did not, in keeping with the prosecution's portrayal of Frances Newton as a monster who preplanned the execution of her family for insurance gain.

The *New York Times* [69] published a veneer-blistering article on Mock's competency regarding another Texas Death Row inmate. The Skeptical Juror, a blog by J. Bennett Allen,[70] states that "[Ron Mock] was the king of bad attorneys," and that of nineteen clients he represented on capital murder charges, sixteen were or are on Death Row. None was acquitted. At one time, a section of Death Row was referred to as "The Mock Wing." After 2001, Mock decided not to pursue capital cases. The Texas Bar Association suspended him twice and placed him on probation three times. As of April 2017, the Texas Bar Association[71] lists Mr. Ronald G. Mock as having been suspended from practicing law in Texas from 2004 to 2007.

The Skeptical Juror rates innocence on a probability scale. He gave Frances Newton 91 percent, one of the highest of two he has given to a Death Row inmate. The 91 percent means Frances had only a 9 percent chance of being guilty. No racial bias appeared in the state's choice of her attorney: Frances Newton is black, and so is Ron Mock; in fact, an overwhelming majority of Mock's Death Row clients are or were black.

In the punishment phase of Frances' trial, the state hired Covert, a psychiatrist, as its prophet for the special issue question: "Is there a probability that the defendant would commit acts of violence that would constitute a continuing threat to society?" Frances Newton was not a violent person; she had just one conviction for forgery. Covert never interviewed Frances and never talked to her. He ascended to the witness stand and answered questions on a hypothetical case, describing Frances as seen through the eyes of the prosecution, and he then was asked to visualize her in the future. Covert stated that this hypothetical case indeed would have a probability of committing acts of violence in the future. The jury returned the death penalty.

For John B. Holmes, Jr., district attorney for Harris County, who also sanctioned the death penalty against Karla Faye and me, this was just another day of business as usual in his department, performing his elected duties to the limit of his ability in keeping with the desires of his constituency: being tough on crime. For opponents of the death penalty, especially their premise of killing the innocent, this was "a date which will live in infamy."[72]

* * *

Frances was a very sweet individual, a very quiet and private, beautiful person. Frances was a Christian when she arrived. In her mugshot, I think you can tell this when you compare hers to the before-salvation mugshots of Karla Faye Tucker and Betty Lou Beets. Frances loved her family and never wavered from her position of innocence. Her prayers always included a plea that they would find the real killers.

Frances Elaine Newton, mugshot, 1988

And now there were four on Female Death Row, Mountain View Unit, Gatesville, Texas, Texas Department of Criminal Justice: Betty Lou, Karla Faye, Frances, and me.

CHAPTER 15

As I had taught Karla Faye and Betty Lou to knit and crochet, so I passed this gift on to Frances. It was an honor to pass this gift to women as it had been passed to me from Ms. Jones, who worked in the kitchen at Juvenile Hall in California, a lifetime away, when I was running from foster homes.

We now had a regular "production line" to make Parole Pal dolls. I can't remember if Betty Lou didn't want to join us the day the picture below was taken or if she was away attending a hearing. As I mentioned, Betty Lou preferred the company of men to women; she was a real loner.

Parole Pal dolls

Making Parole Pal dolls, quilts, afghans, and other arts and crafts was available in a Death Row work capable program known as Special Projects. If you were work capable, you could spend six to eight hours a day in Special Projects and also get two hours per day in the rec room; but if you were not work capable, you got only one hour. If you were not in the Psych Center or in Ad Seg, you were work capable, but you could elect not to join the program. The program was a product of the David Ruíz lawsuit, *Ruíz v. Estelle*.[73]

* * *

No one—not one inmate or employee of TDCJ— with any tenure in the Texas prison system has not heard of David Ruíz[74, 75] and the volcanic civil action case filed June 1972 in the U.S. District Court for the Eastern District of Texas, Tyler Division, C.A. [Civil Action] No. 5523, a *pro se* (for one's own behalf), handwritten writ requesting injunctive relief for confinement conditions that violated his constitutional rights, specifically, the Eighth and Fourteenth Amendments regarding cruel and unusual punishment and due process. When the ash settled eight years later under *Ruíz v. Estelle*,[73, 80] the Texas prison system (then known as TDC, Texas Department of Corrections) changed dramatically—mostly for the good and some for the very bad through unexpected consequences.

The trial lasted 159 days, involved 1,546 exhibits, heard testimony from 349 witnesses, included multiple horror stories of man's inhumanity toward man, and ended with the TDC coming under federal oversight. The issues in *Ruíz v. Estelle* were:

1) Failing or refusing to provide inmates with a medical care delivery system which is accessible and adequate to meet their medical needs;

2) Failing or refusing to provide living and working conditions which do not jeopardize the health and safety of inmates;

3) Failing or refusing to provide inmates with reasonable protection from physical assault;

4) Failing or refusing to permit inmates reasonable access to the courts and to public officials for redress of grievances;

5) Failing or refusing to supervise and control prison officials and employees sufficiently to prevent the systematic imposition of summary and other cruel and unusual punishment on inmates and the systematic denial of due process to inmates.

Legal tremors and eruptions from the Ruíz-instigated judgment continued for another twenty-two years, finally bringing the longest prison lawsuit to a close in 2002, a total of thirty years from inception.

David Resendez Ruíz originated from the east side of Austin, Texas, but spent most of his early life and education, beginning at age twelve, in Gatesville, Texas—The Gatesville State School for Boys in its Mountain View Unit for incorrigibles, which, as noted, now currently houses female Death Row. Ruíz completed four separate terms of lower education through Gatesville, with thirteen attempted escapes. Clearly David Ruíz had an authority problem; perhaps his middle initial, R, should have stood for *Rebel.* In 1959, Ruíz graduated from Gatesville because he had reached the adult age of seventeen. After a short hiatus on the outside, he "applied" for a higher "twelve-year degree" at Huntsville Penitentiary, where he was readily admitted based upon his most recent aptitude for auto theft.

At that time, TDC used the control model for prisons. TDC expected a prisoner to follow all the rules and do his time—to be under control. If he talked back or slacked on his job, punishment might be a severe beating, sometimes to his death, or an extended stay in "the hole," solitary confinement, subsisting on nothing but bread and water. It was absolute control: break his spirit, drive out his criminal propensities, and make him never-ever-ever do anything to come back to TDC. TDC was an economical and self-sufficient system. The control method avoided the cost of hiring an inordinate number of guards by using building tenders, convicts chosen by the warden, to run the cellblocks. Building tenders received special privileges such as having their cell doors unlocked, eating their meals in private, etc. They had brutal, punitive powers that they used freely. In turn, the building tenders selected other inmates to enforce their rule. They corralled the inmates into forced labor (picking cotton, hoeing vegetables, etc.) under the hot Texas sun for ten hours a day—all *de facto* slave labor, as noted, making the TDC system economically self-sufficient. It was a quiet and surface-peaceful operation.

Muckrakers and jailhouse lawyers were discouraged; politicians loved the low cost. People on the outside figured that a convict reaped what he sowed; little did they know this was also literal. A child's parent might make a prophetic remark when they saw prisoners in stripes working on a chain gang by the side of a road, but no one knew the inmates' plight. No one cared. Don't rock any boats. Rehabilitation and education were encouraged—if your skin pigment permitted it.

Although accustomed to stoop labor, Ruíz found the "employment" at TDC insufferable. He rebelled. On one occasion, he stabbed a building tender; on another, he axed a fellow convict. He was periodically beaten and thrown into the hole. After seven years, Ruíz entered the free world for a brief thirteen-month sabbatical. He returned, this time to the Eastham Unit, for a twenty-five-year "advanced degree." He tried to escape only to be caught, beaten, and tossed into the hole for forty-five days on bread and water. Twenty pounds lighter, he had had enough of the TDC work ethic. He cut his Achilles tendons on both ankles. Known as heel-stringing, this exempted him from the heavy work.

Alternating between the infirmary and the hole, Ruíz met his mentor, David Cruz, known in the TDC system as a writ-writer, a jailhouse lawyer. Ruíz's objects of rebellion soon transferred to the system per se rather than to those in the system. He switched from a rebel without a cause to one *with* a cause. The TDC control model was bound to fall; it was just a matter of time and the right people. The *right* people came in the form of some New York lawyers and Judge William Wayne Justice—indeed, that was his last name. Judge Justice, Eastern District Federal Court, was nominated by Texas Senator Ralph Yarborough and appointed by President Lyndon Johnson. If you are looking for a charge of premeditated murder, mention Yarborough, LBJ, and Judge Justice in front of a senior Texas good-ol'-boy, and he will probably die of a coronary, gasping his last while yelling something about "liberal, pinko communists." Many consider that the efforts of these three person-ages, amongst several others, marked the beginning of the end of the Democratic Party's domination in Texas as of this publication.

Ruíz became the lead plaintiff along with seven other inmates in a writ for civil rights violations under section 1983 of the long-forgotten Civil Rights Act of 1889—yes, 1889, and this is not a typographical error. Judge Justice was the activist engine dictating which cars joined his train as plaintiff lawyers and convict plaintiffs; he requested the U.S. Justice Department to couple its engine as *amicus curiae* (friend of the court), later entered as plaintiff-intervenor.

John Hill, the attorney general of Texas under Governor Bill Clements and his staff, fought back with every drop of legal ink they could place on paper for lawsuits, countersuits, stays, delays, and argumentative obfuscations. One of the most memorable actions was a motion for a change of venue from the Eastern District to the Southern District Court in Houston. To their chagrin, Judge Justice merely followed and moved to Houston. No recalcitrant Texas caboose was about to derail his train to prison reform. A fascinating book that details the legal case, the people involved, and interviews with David Ruíz appears in Appendix B.[76]

Mark White[77] was the secretary of state during the filing of the Ruíz Case, and John Hill was the attorney general. Hill put together a legal army dedicated to fight the intrusion on a system that had been successful for years. Their position was that Texas was *not* running an unconstitutionally cruel system. Mark White became the attorney general for the State of Texas in 1979. He followed the battle plan of his predecessor, Hill, and retained the same army that had begun the fight. For years, Texas had very few violent inmate-on-inmate deaths, no more than one every several years. Mark White often remarked, "You might say that you were abused; but I can't look at you and tell that without a physical examination. But I can look at you and tell whether you are dead or alive."

White also stated that he did agree with the concept behind the district court's decisions that Texas was not doing as good a job as it could have. Governor Clements, who had been supportive of Hill's prior defense, turned on White and hollered irresponsibility, lack of effectiveness, etc. But White had announced that he planned to challenge Clements for the governorship. White then called a meeting of the Texas Prison Board—all of whose members had been appointed by Clements—to tell them his legal defense plan and to tour the Walls Unit in Huntsville. There in the infirmary, White noticed a warren of dust and lint bunnies under every bed.

"Why hasn't someone cleaned up all this lint? I can't win a lawsuit unless I have some facts in our favor," he said.

A member of the prison board responded, "We don't have the staff to do that."

"Then why don't you get that fellow out front who is shining the bars on this prison to come up here and shine these floors? They are suing us for dirty floors, not dirty bars."

In spite of the lackadaisical approach of Clements' prison board, White felt they did the best job possible under difficult circumstances and were able to eliminate some of the excessive terms of the Ruíz decision, such as the idealistic impossibility of a single cell for every prisoner. But like so many changes made by man with his bottomless wisdom, what little good that comes always comes mixed with the bad. Regarding the bad, and unfortunately the very bad, as White states: "The removal of the building tenders left a power vacuum." Not only does nature abhor a vacuum, but prisons abhor the vacuum left by a lack of hierarchy, a hierarchy soon replaced by ethnic gangs: the Aryan Brotherhood, Barrio Azteca, Black Guerrilla Family, and the list grows daily.

White stated, "Immediately in this power vacuum, inmate murders occurred almost on a daily basis. The strong began attacking the weak. These violent deaths did not stop until I defeated Bill Clements for governor and through the Texas Prison Board obtained a new director of TDCJ. After that, inmate deaths did subside."

Most TDCJ employees and Texas citizens blame Ruíz personally for the resultant gang problems. They revile him and are quick to point out that he was anything but a Boy Scout, that he was a thief, a crook, and had a history of being capable of murder. But regarding his dramatic contribution to changing inhumane conditions in the Texas prison system, Ruíz summed it up most poignantly in an article in *The Austin Chronicle*: "We are still human beings and should be treated in a humane manner, and there are laws supporting that. I never asked for a Holiday Inn. I asked to be treated as a human being."[78]

Pragmatically, the Ruíz decision created the prison gang situation, but looking closer, perhaps it was the result of the lack of an adequate number of guards, the lack of comprehensive rehabilitation, the lack of separating mental-health issues from criminal confinement, the lack of separating narcotic addictions from criminal confinement, the lack of…*ad nauseam*…and all in turn stemming from the lack of adequate funding.

Ruíz died in prison in November 2005 from liver cancer allowed to grow unchecked from its first noted discovery in 2002.[79] He left a documented report on how he died from medical neglect.

* * *

The work capable program for female Death Row inmates coming from *Ruíz v. Estelle* was a godsend. It gave us a respite and time to commune with each other. I corresponded with David Ruíz for many years. He was a big help to me on my appeals, giving me a lot of legal information on my case. When I entered the Harris County Jail for my first trial, there were thirteen women there under federal protection to testify for the *Ruíz v. Estelle* lawsuit. I befriended several of them, and that is where I first heard of David Ruíz. After my sentence and departure to Death

Row at Goree, Linda Burnett, the only other woman on Death Row at that time, mentioned David Ruíz. She was regularly corresponding with David and wrote to him about me. I got a letter from him. He told me who he was and that there would be many changes in the prison system. Also, that if there was anything he could do to help me with my case, to just ask. I did ask, in a number of letters. David accurately foretold that I would get a retrial because of the vacillating juror, Mr. John O. Vennard. And soon there were noticeable changes that I could see, just as David had predicted. Inmates were no longer running the prisons. In the medical area, inmates were no longer taking blood from other inmates. When Karla Faye entered, and I re-entered, Mountain View on Death Row, Karla Faye received a letter from David outlining the new work capable program.

* * *

For about seven years, an uneasy peace surrounded us in Death Row. There were just the four of us making Prison Pal dolls and communing together in our Lord. This photo shows us praising our Savior around Christmastime.

Left to right: Karla Faye Tucker, Betty Lou Beets, Pamela Lynn Perillo,
Frances Elaine Newton

No, this is not jailhouse religion; these are four women praising God, four daughters in Christ who know they have sinned and are forgiven, perhaps not by those on earth whom we have sinned against. For those, we are praying that God will comfort them and know we are repentant. We beg for their forgiveness, and by the Holy Spirit, the wind whose direction we cannot discern, this often happens. The brother of Deborah Thornton, the young girl whom Karla Faye and Danny Garrett killed, converted to Christianity and indeed forgave Karla Faye. He later actively protested not only Karla Faye's death penalty but the whole concept in general. During this period, Karla Faye and I both got our GEDs. We also took some college courses by correspondence.

I liken this seven-year period to a quiet and deep pool beneath a spreading, tree-covered bank. It's peaceful, shady, and cool, but mainly on the surface; beneath the gentle dimples that ripple across her silver sheet lurk beasts of prey. And in the sky soar heaven-forgiven sins that our flesh cannot forget. During this period, our appeals went out and returned, soon to be covered in tears as they were always denied. We came together in a circle and prayed over them, and there were always a few crumbs of hope in each appellate decision that nourished us. Uplifted, we returned to our peaceful pool, resting and waiting.

One of the first of my disappointing appellate decisions came in 1988. In any death-sentence case, a petition to the Texas Court of Criminal Appeals is automatic. William Burge, who was my attorney in my first trial, and who obtained the appeal granting my second trial, also handled this direct appeal. In this, he first pointed out my "ineffective assistance of counsel" in Jim Skelton and all of his shenanigans during the trial, especially his relationship with Linda Fletcher. This fact was, to others and to me, the worst error in this trial. There were five points of error that Burge raised, but this one should have been our game-winning point.

Another error raised was that of another "vacillating juror," venireperson Griggs. Mrs. Griggs's testimony during *voir dire* was similar to that of venireperson Vennard in my first trial. As noted, Mr. Vennard in my first trial was the angel in disguise that, in effect, gave me my second trial. Of these five points of error, the other three were legal points that I am not sure I understood. The other two so noted were the most important, especially the incompetence of Skelton. On all five points, however, the Texas court overruled every ground for error.

In 1993, Danny Garrett, Karla Faye's fall partner, cheated the state and died of cirrhosis of the liver. All the years of bartending with free samples must have had their toll. Karla Faye said she felt a real sadness in his passing. She had always felt remorse for testifying against him and his receiving the death penalty.

My adopted mother, Christina, and her husband paid an attorney to file my next appeal, a writ of *habeas corpus* to the Fifth Circuit of the United States Court of Appeals with the main item regarding wrongful conviction being, of course, Skelton's conflict of interest in also representing Linda Fletcher. The U.S. Court of Appeals refused to allow any discovery or evidentiary hearing, thus upholding my death sentence.

Latin for "you have the body," "*habeas corpus* is a writ that is used to bring a party criminally convicted in state court into federal court. Usually, writs of *habeas corpus* review the legality of the party's arrest, imprisonment, or detention. The federal court's review of a *habeas corpus* petition is considered to be collateral relief of a state court decision rather than direct review."[81] The federal court is not going to review a case for errors of procedure, interpretation, etc., but will look only for violations of federal law. In 1995-96, the U.S. Congress changed the procedure for writs of *habeas corpus* in death penalty cases in order to curtail the number of frivolously repeated appeals whereby an inmate could delay the death penalty for years.[82] The point that during those years evidence might surface to prove that the inmate was innocent did not seem to bother those who are pro-death and those who vote for D.A.s, judges, and governors pledging to get tough on crime. Rather than pass a law to exclude frivolous appeals, they took the approach my mother had so many years before and punished everyone. Texas also devised a unique and overkill procedure to limit writs of *habeas corpus* (WHCs). Before the inmate can file in a district court, he must file and subsequently be denied in the Texas Court of Criminal Appeals. So they simply limited the Texas court appeal to one and only one. I know that Divine timing allowed me to squeeze through this closing door and continue my appeals.

I felt badly about Christina's paying the attorneys for my appeals. She had done and was doing so much already in raising my son. I wrote the Texas State Bar Association and said that I was on Death Row and desperately needed an appellate attorney.[82] They placed my name on a list, and Baker Botts,[83] a well-known and well-respected global firm with headquarters in Houston, chose me as one of its two *pro bono* Death Row cases. Choosing two cases at a time, they work on those two until they are finished. Throughout their counsel, I always had five very competent attorneys. I felt so blessed when they chose me. I had hope.

CHAPTER 16

Mike Barber of Mike Barber Prison Ministries, whom I mentioned earlier as doing so much for me, also did so much for Karla Faye, who was party to a miracle. In 1992, Mike introduced Karla Faye to a fellow minister, Dana Brown. Shortly afterward, Karla Faye became smitten, but she knew it wasn't in her situation to fall in love. Nonetheless, she prayed, and God, who always answers, this time said, "Yes." Soon, Dana Brown and Karla Faye were a couple, a couple made in heaven, sharing a spiritual love, profound and eternal. Dana proposed in 1994. Unusual in a Death Row situation, but not impossible, they set a prison marriage date. Karla Faye planned to be a June bride in 1995, married by proxy.

During this joyous and festive time, Karla Faye, with her usual charisma, seemed to levitate our cellblock into the clouds. She planned every detail, including a perfectly coordinated service. Dana was in a hotel in Waco, Texas, with a staff chaplain; I stood in for Dana at Gatesville, and Frances Newton stood in for the minister. At the precise moment that Dana finished his vows, Karla Faye repeated hers and then shed a tear of joy. All eyes glistened, including those of Linda Strom, a prison minister who was also present. In *Karla Faye Tucker Set Free*, Strom[84] gives a soul-rending account of Dana and Karla Faye's love and marriage. (Strom also can be credited for pointing out to Karla Faye the telephone-pole "crosses" that could be seen from her window.) Years later in September 2013 under House Bill 869, Texas banned proxy weddings for inmates,[85] but at this point in God-ordained time, an "agape" marriage did indeed occur.

* * *

After the legal firm of Baker Botts took on my case, the State of Texas, noting that my first appeal to the Fifth Circuit had been denied, concluded that the appellate process was exhausted and requested my presence in that all-too-familiar place, the 248th Criminal District Court, Houston. There, they would set a formal and final execution date. A Roman Colosseum affair, I knew there would be lots of TV cameras, reporters, and others with nothing better to do than ogle. Consequently, I didn't want anyone there except my adopted mom, Christina. I especially did not want my son there, because I had been very protective of him against the media. Joseph was now in senior high and had all the right values. I was so proud of him. I didn't want the media pestering him and judging him in the press for my past actions. But Joseph insisted on coming.

"Mom, I am going to be there. I want to be there for you."

"Okay," I said, "but don't acknowledge who I am. I'm not going to look at you. Don't let the media know that you are someone there for me."

Like a staged play, the judge asked me to rise. I don't remember the exact words, but they were something to the effect of, "Before such and such a time, you will be delivered to the Walls Unit in Huntsville, Texas. You have been sentenced to die by twelve of your peers, and you will die on such and such a date by lethal injection. May God have mercy on your soul."

Then there was the rumble of voices, feet hitting the floor, and the show was over except, of course, for the falderal I knew would take place in the theater lobby, the hallway outside the courtroom. I also knew the judge's words would have upset Joseph, so as we were wedging a path through cameramen and reporters to get on the elevator, I turned to my son and was about to wink at him (contrary to my prior edict), to let him know that everything was all right. In a microsecond, one of the reporters, with the innate sense of a coyote smelling the blood of a wounded rabbit from miles away, pirouetted and pegged his camera on Joseph. At the same moment, Robin Curtis, one of my first attorneys with Baker Botts, wheeled upon the reporter, pushed his camera away, and said, "He is a minor. If you show him on the news, we will have a lawsuit against you so fast your head will spin off." Robin Curtis was young and feisty. I always likened her to "a little hell on wheels." There was no mention of my son on TV.

With my execution date set for September 12, 1995, the argument of whether Chipita Rodriguez or Jane Elkins was the last woman executed in Texas in the mid-1850s meant little to me. All I knew was that I was next in line. Why shouldn't I be "the first"? I had been here on Death Row the longest.

Many tears. Many prayers. The little rock dam at the end of our quiet seven-year pool of peace was crumbling; generally slow waters were now emptying rapidly into a rock-strewn river where rapids and falls churned the emotions. Then the sharks appeared and moved around me in a giant circle. A blood scent was in the waters, the chum of a sensational gory-story and possibly a movie. Since I was to be the first woman executed in almost 150 years, *everyone* wanted the exclusive rights to my story. They were like bugs crawling out of the woodwork—Houstonian cockroaches at the old Harris County Jail on Franklin Street. HBO[86] wanted to film me right up to the execution. Of course, they couldn't film the actual execution. If they could have, I am sure they would have. They wanted to capture me on a daily basis sharing how I was feeling, what was going through my mind, and what was going to happen next. No! No!

Shortly after my return to Mountain View Death Row, Larry Fitzgerald, and another man—I think his last name was Neeley (from the marketing department at Mountain View, which handled interviews)—approached me.

"Pamela, we have a real good friend named Michael Graczyk who would like to interview you. We know that he will be fair with you. Would you reconsider your position about not granting interviews this one time...uh...under these conditions?"[87]

"Yes, I suppose," I replied. It was the one and only time I would grant an interview aside from those related to this book, and I think I did so because I was tired of being picked over like a dead animal by the side of the road.

Michael was fair as promised. This is our conversation as best I can remember: I told him, "Anyone on Death Row is no longer treated as a person when it comes near the end. The media hounds them for exclusive rights to their story, for intensive interviews, and this is the reason I haven't allowed any in the past."

I said, "I will be at peace when the execution goes through…I am tired of the emotional roller coaster, in and out of the courts, where one court gives you a reprieve and the next shoots you down. You might get a stay of execution one place, and then two weeks later they set another date. I'm tired…At this point, I am at peace. I know I will see Jesus. I am ready."

We talked about my crime and my trials. I told him, "It was a horrible thing to do, and I leave with all compassion for what I did to the families involved and will beg their forgiveness as I leave. I still feel…I don't know the exact words…miffed or concerned that my fall partner, Linda Briddle, who was also very much involved, only received five years' probation. Also that my attorney, Jim Skelton, obviously had other things going with Linda that were detrimental to my second trial, and the State of Texas refused to look into the matter.

"In the end, you are looked at like a piece of meat instead of a human. Everybody wants a piece of the meat so they can make money. In the end, when you're trying to focus quietly on getting ready to meet your Lord, here comes the whole nation, flapping and pecking for what they can shred off, exclusives and interviews, quotes for their sensational books."

And then, another miracle: In July, my attorney at Baker Botts obtained a stay of execution through the Fifth Circuit of Appeals, a stay that delayed the execution until they could review the case more closely. *Hallelujah! God must be sparing me for something,* I thought.

Then turbulent water again: The TDCJ introduced a smoking ban for all Texas prisons.[88] At age forty and after almost thirty years of cigarettes and at a time of high stress, no more smokes. For those who have tried to stop smoking, one of the hardest struggles is when others around you *are* smoking. At least with a total ban, that could not happen.

About this time, I got a letter from Mike Briddle, my fall partner. The TDCJ still allowed us to correspond with other inmates in 1995. I didn't like Mike when I first met him in California, and I didn't like him on our three-week crime spree. We fought a lot because of his philosophy that women existed merely to turn tricks and bring in money. During our trip, Linda Briddle (now Linda Fletcher)—reluctantly—became the only pony in his stable. I found a different side to Mike after he exhausted all of his appeals and the State set his execution date for the end of the year. Mike was, as noted, extremely prejudiced and an ardent and aggressive member of the Aryan Brotherhood. He had a daughter from his first marriage, the one before his marriage to Linda, a daughter whom he dearly loved. To Mike's complete loathing, she had a baby by a black man and another by a Mexican man. He disowned her and never spoke to her afterward. However, with an execution pending, he called home to say goodbye. His five-year-old granddaughter answered the phone and, by means unknown, knew who he was and said, "Paw-Paw?" Mike wrote that when he heard her call him Paw-Paw, all the things he'd believed in just melted, and he finally knew what "unconditional love" meant. He wrote that he couldn't believe how so much hatred could just vanish in the instant that he heard her voice. He got out of the Aryan Brotherhood and renounced their neo-Nazi, Godless religion.

Mike was a Catholic in his youth. His chaplain called our chaplain, who told me that in the end, Mike found peace and had a priest give him the last rites. His final absolution was a personal blessing to me because I had written to Mike so many times and tried to tell him about our Lord and His peace through forgiveness, but Mike wanted nothing to do with it. Mike was executed December 12, 1995. He declined to make a last statement. I felt a lot of sadness for Mike—a life lost in hatred, a life that, based on hints from his final actions, could have been filled with love.

CHAPTER 17

Two, Three, One, Two, Six, Eight, Three, Four, Five, Six, Seven...

A numbers game? Perhaps an IQ test to determine the next logical number in succession? No, just my history on Death Row. I started in the Goree Unit as one of *two* that were condemned in a *three*-person cellblock. From there, I entered the Mountain View Unit into a *six*-person cellblock where I became the number *one*. Next there were *two* of us, Karla Faye and me; then we moved to an *eight*-cell unit to make it *three* and *four*: Karla Faye, Betty, Frances, and me. In 1995, we received numbers *five, six,* and *seven*: Erica Sheppard, Cathy Lynn Henderson, and Darlie Routier. There might not be any logical mathematical progression for these numbers, but the number of unoccupied Death Row cells always increased before an increase in the number of female inmates—always maintaining a surplus. Maybe Texas foresaw another possible federal lawsuit because the state was executing a far lower ratio of women compared to men.[89]

In 1996, I received a letter in the mail notifying me that Judge Curt F. Steib in a Texas district court had denied my *habeas corpus* appeal. My appeal was, of course, predicated upon the serpentine actions of my two-faced attorney, Jim Skelton. My attorneys, Gerard Desrochers and Robin Curtis with Baker Botts, immediately filed an appeal with the U.S. Court of Appeals, Fifth District. They not only noted Skelton's actions but also pointed out that Judge Steib's review was just a paper hearing and was not, by other factors, entitled to the presumption of correctness. The state continued forward, and I received my second execution date: March 24, 1996.

I was scheduled for lethal injection on a Sunday at 12:01 a.m. On a Sunday, the day of our Lord, ironically, Texas would finally execute a female and send her to be with her Lord. TDCJ sends women, "those about to die," to the Goree Unit located a few miles from the Walls Unit in Huntsville. There they stay for a few days and are "prepared" for execution. All executions, male and female, take place at the Walls Unit. The Ellis Unit houses male Death Row inmates and is also their place of preparation. Three days prior to my transport to Goree, my adopted mom and my son arrived in Gatesville. They stayed at a motel, and Warden Baggett, out of kindness, let us have contact visits those final three days.

On Thursday, Warden Baggett talked with us about the TDCJ protocol package. The protocol package contains all the morbid details regarding the execution: what color clothes you will wear at your death, where your family will collect your body, to whom you will leave any property and any money left in your prison account (a last will and testament), and whom you will choose for the five witnesses to watch you die.

The state may have five witnesses and the condemned, also five. The adjoining viewing rooms for the witnesses are, of course, separate. That for the state, which may include the victim's family, is closer to the head of the gurney. After the condemned has been prepped (strapped down with five leather belts, IV started, arms strapped and extended on sideboards in a crucifixion pose, etc.), the witnesses enter the viewing rooms. A draw curtain is pulled back, revealing a plate-glass window covered with vertical and horizontal bars in a tic-tac-toe pattern. If you wanted to, you could raise your head from the death gurney and see who is cheering and who is crying as you prepare for your last gasp. There is also a witness room for the press. I did not know if Michael Graczyk would be there or not. Linda Strom, who wrote *Karla Faye Tucker Set Free*, was one of my witnesses. I did not put my son or adopted mother on the witness list. I *did not* want them watching me die. Of course, none of my family from California would be there. Warden Baggett allowed a correctional officer, Ms. Scott, to accompany me and sit outside the death-watch cell. Ms. Scott also agreed to be one of my witnesses. She said, "Pam, this will be very hard for me, but I will do it if the warden allows it," which she did. These were the only two I had chosen to witness my death.

I didn't have in writing what my final words would be, but I knew what I would talk about: that I knew I would be with Jesus, and I knew I would see Karla Faye again when she joined me. I would turn the actual words over to God.

On Thursday evening after my son and adopted mother left, I was in turmoil. My death was scheduled in three days. I felt a lot of fear. It wasn't a fear of dying, because I knew I would go to heaven and meet Jesus face to face. It was more of a fear, rather an anxiety, of being strapped to that gurney and having to say my last words with all those people watching me die. Then a feeling of guilt followed this because, as a Christian, I knew I shouldn't have fear. Subsequently, the feeling of guilt turned inward as anger at myself for feeling such, but then I reflected on Jesus in the Garden of Gethsemane before His crucifixion. In His anxiety, He sweated drops of blood and prayed to His Father, "...if it is possible, may this cup be taken from me. Yet not as I will, but as you will."[90] At last I was comforted because He had come down in the flesh and I, being also flesh on bone, had felt His fear. In that passage, He showed me it was okay. From that point on, I prayed that God would give me the strength to walk into that room with my head held high, to get up on that gurney and say I was sorry to the family of my victims, and to say that I was going home to be with Jesus.

That night as I was flipping through my Bible in the book of Psalms—I had been reading a lot from Psalms at that time—I happened on Psalms 102:19, 20 (NIV): "The Lord looked down from his sanctuary on high, from Heaven He viewed the earth, to hear the groans of the prisoners and release those condemned to death." I've read my Bible through many times and don't remember seeing this passage, and yet these verses seemed to jump from the page into my very being—the living word, *Rhema*[91]—comfort to my soul. I slept in peace, a peace that encompassed my whole body, physically, mentally, and spiritually. Knowing that either way God decided, if I departed, my reward would be with Jesus, and if I stayed, He had a purpose for me here.

The next morning, a Friday, I told Christina and Joseph goodbye in an emotional embrace. Later that day, TDCJ would transport me to Huntsville for my appointed execution at one minute into Sunday.

As I was walking out the door, I received notice of a telephone call from my attorneys saying that I had received a stay of execution and a rehearing. I returned to the visiting room to tell Christina and Joseph. Tears of goodbye were now tears of hallelujah—an unforgettable emotional upheaval that I will never forget.

CHAPTER 18

Two primary states of waiting occur on Death Row: waiting for the state to finalize the appointed day of your execution and waiting for that day, once known, to come. Waiting to find out when is akin to closing the closet door in your bedroom when you were a little girl and placing a chair in front of it to try to protect yourself from something lurking outside. Surely that would keep the bogeyman away while you slept, even though you knew he was in there. You knew he had earthly, manmade powers to tear down any barrier. You knew he was plotting to get you. You also knew, however, that the day of his re-entry was random; it could be in several weeks or many years. Such was my wait after the stay of execution.

In March 1996, the U.S. Court of Appeals, Fifth Circuit,[92] vacated the state court's dismissal of my *habeas corpus* petition and remanded my case for "appropriate discovery and an evidentiary hearing." An evidentiary hearing after a conviction occurs before a judge without a jury present to determine if certain evidence not presented at trial needs consideration, evidence that would require a retrial. Our primary point for retrial was, of course, the conflict of interest pertaining to my attorney, Jim Skelton. That November, the court held its first evidentiary hearing, consisting largely of affidavits and exhibits from Skelton and others involved in both of my trials. On August 5, 1997, the court denied my *habeas corpus* relief. My state of waiting became gloomy again until one day later, when one of my attorneys called.

"Jim Skelton has been disbarred and is no longer able to practice law in the state of Texas. He lied to a client about his status on a federal conviction appeal, when the court dismissed his client's appeal long before Skelton told him about a fictitious oral argument. Unfortunately for Mr. Skelton's defense, his client had tape recordings to back it up.

We will be filing an appeal for a new evidentiary hearing based on this *new* evidence, namely Mr. Skelton's lack of credibility."

Words and phrases from old sayings ran through my mind like school children galloping out for recess—phrases like "chickens roosting," "pants on fire," "shooting yourself in the foot," "what goes around comes around," "given enough rope," etc. Hallelujah! The truth had come out into the light. This should be called the third state of waiting, or better titled "hope":

1) Hope for new evidence and a retrial (for Karla Faye, Betty Lou, and certainly now in my case);

2) Hope for a confession from the real killer (in Frances' case); and

3) Hope for clemency, a commutation to life imprisonment from the governor (for all of us nearing the final moment).

Then, almost a year later, after my stay in 1996, Karla Faye's wait for the appointed day ended when the U.S. Court of Appeals, Fifth Circuit, ruled against her rehearing. Her appeals exhausted, the state set her execution for early the next year, February 3, 1998. We felt immense sorrow for Karla Faye—dejection—but we came together, joined hands, and prayed in emphasis of our belief that we were "…cast down, but not destroyed."[93] I would not let Karla Faye fade quietly away, and certainly Karla Faye herself wasn't going out without letting the world know what "born again" meant. I wrote to Sister Helen Prejean (the death penalty opponent of *Dead Man Walking* fame)[94] to let her know that she needed to come here and fight for Karla Faye Tucker, one of God's most dramatic salvations.

When Sister Helen arrived, she, Karla Faye, and I sat in the prison chapel for an hour and talked. She described her efforts and travels over the world to denounce the death penalty. I will never forget her saying, "Is it right to kill people to show people that killing is wrong?" And also, "Even an officer who handcuffs you and escorts you to the van that takes you to your execution is taking a part in your death." She pledged to do everything she could for Karla Faye's cause and mine as well. The call went out to petition then-governor, now former U.S. President, George W. Bush for clemency.

In the next few months, Karla Faye escalated from being a famous person to a very famous person. Not only was she to be the first female executed in over one hundred years, she was a poster child for redemption in Jesus. The reporters and writers swarmed in so heavily for interviews that some of the girls complained about all the media coming into Death Row and taking over the recreation room. They had also complained about our four (Karla Faye, Betty Lou, Frances, and me) commandeering the rec room for Bible study with groups like Mike Barber Ministries and the Bill Glass Crusade for Life.[95] All it took was one Death Row inmate to block the entrance of the media or a ministry. For more than a decade, the four of us had been a tight family group, our own little island. Now the river of time was changing its course. The loss of our prayer and study groups was most upsetting. Karla Faye wanted some privacy, some place where she could be alone and commune with her Lord. With Warden Baggett's permission, she transferred over to MPF (the MultiPurpose Facility) on November 17, 1997. Since Karla Faye's birthday was on the 18th, Warden Baggett let us have a small party for her before she left. Warden Baggett also allowed Frances and me to meet with Karla Faye every two weeks in the visiting area at MPF for about an hour. Betty Lou didn't join us.

It was in MPF that Larry King[96] did his live interview with Karla Faye in January, less than a month before her execution. We were able to see the broadcast live, and I have its transcript, which does follow the show accurately. Karla Faye was eloquent, as I knew she would be, in her testimony for Christ. Early into the interview, Larry King delved extensively into Karla Faye's spiritual marriage to Dana Brown and especially—for listener appeal, I am sure—that Death Row prisoners were not allowed contact visits, not even a handshake. Also discussed was the fact that Governor Bush had never pardoned anyone. Clemency was Karla Faye's last hope, for certainly she was "a new creature in Christ" and no longer a threat to society.

Sister Helen[97] states her views—in an altogether unfavorable analysis—as to why Governor Bush refused clemency. In summary, she notes that if he displayed an act of compassion, it would endanger his political aspirations, would not endear him to the pro-death voters, and would encourage all condemned prisoners to claim "born again" as grounds for mercy.

For her last meal, Karla Faye had a banana, a peach, and a garden salad. Perhaps such a light meal might have been to protect her "delicate intestines," as she often said. Relief was a constant problem of Karla Faye's, one that often required an emergency trip to the restroom when in public. She could have ordered just about anything for her last meal, a sort of before-the-fact tradition that has been in existence since ancient times—a symbolic act of truce and mercy offered to the condemned to prevent them from returning to haunt the executioners.[98] Also, many consider it to be symbolic of the Lord's Last Supper.[99, 100]

For her five witnesses, Karla Faye chose Dana Brown, her husband; Kari Weeks, her sister; George Secrest, her lead attorney; Jackie Oncken, a close friend and wife of one of her court-appointed attorneys, Henry Oncken; and—most unusually—Ron Carlson, the brother of Deborah Thornton, one of her two victims. As noted, Ron Carlson had converted to Christianity through contact with Karla. Life is a journey, and the people we touch along the way always amaze me. One never knows the effect of what even our mere presence may have on others. Jesus sums this up in such a beautiful verse: "The wind blows wherever it pleases. You hear its sound, but you cannot tell where it comes from or where it is going. So it is with everyone born of the Spirit."[101]

Former warden Jim Willett[102] was present at the execution and said, "I was at the Huntsville Unit during her execution. For several years while I was the warden at the Diagnostic Unit, I would go over to the Huntsville Unit during executions and be the person who manned a live telephone connection with the attorney general's office in Austin. I'd usually get a call from them just prior to 6 p.m. and stay on the line with the attorney who had that case, until the execution was completed. This was a precautionary position in case something suddenly came out of the courts and to keep the AG's office informed of the proceedings here in Huntsville. This was, without a close comparison, the largest crowd I saw during the years I did this job for Warden Jones. There were several television satellite trucks and hundreds of people out front of the prison. But it was a peaceful crowd."

I believe that Karla Faye may have had a general idea of what she would say for her last statement, but—as she did so often—she turned the actual wording over to the Lord:

"Yes sir, I would like to say to all of you, the Thornton family and Jerry Dean's family, that I am so sorry. I hope God will give you peace with this. Baby, I love you. Ron, give Peggy a hug for me. Everybody has been so good to me. I love all of you very much. I am going to be face to face with Jesus now. Warden Baggett, thank all of you so much. You have been so good to me. I love all of you very much. I will see you all when you get there. I will wait for you."[103]

I have heard that the bond between men is always stronger than that between women. I disagree. Karla Faye and I had been Death Row inmates for over fourteen years. Our bond was not only in the flesh but also like iron in the Spirit. I don't know how many lakes of tears I filled in her passing. I would have gladly gone in her place.

Karla Faye
Pamela Lynn Perillo

A little girl lost
Her world full of pain
He said it feels good
She gave him her vein
The dope made her numb
And the numbness felt free
Until she came down
To a new misery
A junkie, a whore
Living for the next high
She'd lie, cheat, and steal
She forgot how to cry
Wide awake for two weeks
Shooting heroin then speed
When she killed in cold blood
She felt nothing but her need

It's an eye for any eye
Now you're going to die
A tooth for a tooth
It's your moment of truth
There's no mercy here
Your stay is denied
Go ahead and pray
There's no mercy
In the sky

Alone in her cell
No dope in her veins

The killer becomes
The little girl lost again
She fell to her knees
She prayed she would die
On the cold cement floor
She finally cried

And love came like the wind
Love whispered her name
It reached through and held her
It lifted her pain
14 years on death row
Her faith deeper each day
Her last words were
I love you all
Goodbye Karla Faye

Now it's an eye for an eye
And alone you will die
A tooth for a tooth
It's your moment of truth

Karla Faye Tucker, 1959-1998

In May of 1998, shortly after the State of Texas killed my best friend, the district court granted me a second evidentiary hearing. Hopefully, this would be a *full* evidentiary hearing, not just with affidavits, but with the testimonies of real people. From conversations with my attorneys, I learned that this would take time. The bogeyman could be in the closet for several more years.

* * *

In November of the same year, Martin Gurule and six other Death Row inmates escaped from the Ellis Unit outside Huntsville. Martin drowned in a nearby creek, and the hounds quickly corralled the other six. Within six months, the TDCJ moved the male Death Row to a more secure setting at the Polunsky Unit about sixty miles to the east of Huntsville.[104, 105]

This escape and relocation of male Death Row inmates had a strong effect on the six of us remaining on female Death Row. It was quite evident to me that their escape was a demoralizing affront to the TDCJ system. Our imprisonment changed dramatically. They moved all of us to the Multi-Purpose Facility Unit, where Karla Faye had been before leaving for Huntsville. MPF is essentially a psych center for suicidal inmates and those needing regulation for their psychotropic medications. A nurses' station anchored this section from another part that has twelve cells (the new Death Row): six cells on each side of a day room. When Texas added the death penalty for killing a child under ten years of age, I knew Death Row needed more room.

There were eight of us now as Brittany Holberg and Kimberly McCarthy had boarded the death train. Compared to our previous confinement, this was a dungeon. We each occupied a small cell behind a solid steel door. No table, no chair, just a sink, a toilet, and a bed. You ate with your tray on the bed or on one of the fixtures. Room to turn around? Barely. And room to pace? None. Even an animal in a cage at the zoo has room to pace in a circle.

Five of us were no longer work capable and were able to enjoy only one hour of rec per day outside of our cell, rather than two. They scheduled this one-hour rec time so early in the morning that no one wanted to go. Of these five, three chose not to work, and another inmate and I entered Ad Seg on orders from the medical department because of carpal tunnel syndrome; we were not able to work at pulling cotton apart for seven and a half hours and get an extra hour of rec time.

One of the nearby schools brought some newspapers and magazines for us. The general population could read them, but the prison administration decided we couldn't. Another privilege removed. Through the grapevine and letters, we found that the male Death Row inmates had televisions outside their cells along the run and could watch from seven in the morning until eleven at night. We had no televisions; our single chance to watch one was in the rec room during our limited one-hour-per-day visit, two hours if work capable. Strip searches took place at least once, and sometimes as many as eight times, every day, often before and after a time when we never had left our tombs or before and after transporting us from the rec room back to our cells—as if we could materialize something out of the air and hide it on our person when the guards are standing beside us from start to finish.

Surprise cell searches were so frequent that they were hardly a surprise. On one such search, a guard opened a little wooden box that held some of my special pictures in an album, jammed her hand ruthlessly inside the folders, and scattered some of the pictures on the floor. Then she slammed the lid closed, and I saw the metal clasp puncture one picture. When she left, I opened the box and yelled in agony. I started crying. The clasp had gouged a hole in the last picture taken of my deceased daughter, Stephanie, right through her face as she lay in her coffin—the little doll from a different universe with Sammy so many eons ago. Later

I confronted the guard: "You ruined the last picture of my daughter when you slammed the lid down on my lock-box."

"Well, you shouldn't have had it loose in that box," she snarled.

Although I pointed out that it was in an album, she turned away. I then showed it to the lieutenant on our unit, who said, "What do you want me to do about it?" Later, I placed it in an envelope with a note to Warden Baggett. She had it repaired, but you can still see the damage. Nonetheless, I was grateful.

Now I knew exactly how David Ruíz felt when he said he didn't expect the Holiday Inn, but he did expect "to be treated as a human being." The primary punishment phase in the general population section, those who are serving time, is the loss of freedom. In addition to that, Death Row inmates have the punishment of the waiting-to-die status. Certainly that should be enough without harassment and humiliation. There was no reason for all the searches, especially the strip searches, because there had been no instances of misbehavior in our unit.

Consequently, I prepared a To-Whom-It-May-Concern letter in April 1999, outlining these grievances, and published it in the Canadian Coalition Against the Death Penalty (CCADP).[106] The CCADP is a website maintained and updated by Dave Parkinson and Tracy Lamourie and "has offered free web space to over 1,000 Death Row Prisoners Since 1998." I also sent corresponding copies of my letter to Judge William Wayne Justice and Attorney Donna Brorby, the lead attorney for Ruíz, et al. In my letter, I noted the horrible abuse of the mental patients in the section adjoining Death Row, in the Psych Center.

I heard one officer say, "We had to pepper spray that nut three times. She just sat there batting that pepper spray up in the air." I also noted how one inmate had died in the Psych Center. She came here from another unit suffering from internal bleeding, apparently from blunt force trauma. It was a Friday, and there were no doctors available. She was placed in a cell with nothing but a paper gown, no pad, no blanket—nothing. And she just lay there on a cement floor under bright lights. She wouldn't move. She wouldn't eat. That night, on the third shift, the lone officer on duty noticed dark matter oozing from her mouth, nose, and ears, and that she lay in "feces black as tar, which meant it had blood in it." The officer would not open the cell to check on her. She said she needed to have Security present to open a cell. The poor girl lay on the floor of that cell, slowly dripping out her lifeblood, until Monday when the "doctor" (actually a physician's assistant) finally arrived. However, the PA would not see her, and she died on Wednesday. I could hear their conversations, especially the last one when an officer looked in and said, "Oh, my, what happened? She won't wake up." And then I could see with my mirror extended through the bars that the warden and medical personnel were going in and out. Soon, they removed the inmate on a gurney, and we could see the Coryell County ambulance coming in through the back way. The other details I got from a friendly correctional officer.

In the last paragraph of my letter, mostly directed at Justice and Brorby, I specifically asked if we were still under the Ruíz Death Row Activity Plan or were "these people" no longer under this court order? Brorby did answer, "Judge Justice has released federal oversight on the TDCJ for all matters except the medical and mental health and retardation (MHR) issues." In order to satisfy their legal obligations, the TDCJ fired two nurses and a doctor, which I suppose was nothing more than sacrificing a few scapegoats.

In October, Suzanne Margaret Basso joined us, bringing the total condemned to nine. In November, I sent a sworn affidavit summarizing this April letter to Amnesty International published by Deja.com, a group absorbed by Google, Inc., some years later.[(107)] I had now been on Death Row for nineteen years. I was still clinging to my prayer-requested hope on the forthcoming evidentiary hearing.

CHAPTER 20

I was not present at my second evidentiary hearing, but I heard the details by telephone from my attorneys at Baker Botts. I wish I had been there to see the brightness inside the courtroom, because the truth did come out in the light. We had new evidence regarding my Sixth Amendment right to "effective assistance of conflict-free counsel at trial," namely, further exposure into the credibility of my court–appointed attorney, Jim Skelton. This hearing was a full evidentiary hearing with verbal testimony. First presented at this hearing was the fact that the State Bar of Texas disbarred Skelton in 1997 regarding his failure to respond to a grievance filed against him. In this grievance, Steve Garza, a former police officer in federal prison for "conspiracy to possess cocaine with intent to distribute"[108] paid Skelton—I believe it was ten thousand dollars—to file a motion for appeal. Skelton told Garza that he had presented an oral argument to an "interested" Fifth Circuit panel, and Garza's conviction had been affirmed on appeal. No wiggle room here—a tape recording confirmed this conversation. In truth, no such oral argument ever occurred, and Garza's appeal had been dismissed for "want of prosecution" months before Skelton told Garza of the fictitious argument and affirmation. With less legalese, Skelton did not perform on behalf of his client and lied to him about doing so. After presenting this material, Skelton took the stand. "Have you ever lied to your clients?" He responded, "If I have to, I will."

I understand that Robert Pelton, Skelton's former law partner and co-counsel in my second trial, also took the stand. When the judge asked him, "Did you at any time during the trial in question tell Mr. Skelton that you felt that it was a conflict of interest for him to represent Ms. Perillo?"

"Yes," he responded, "I told him that it was my opinion that his relationship with Linda Fletcher had developed a conflict of interest in his representation of Perillo, and further, that it was unethical."

These two testimonies emphasized Skelton's lack of credibility and his conflict of interest with respect to his relationship with Linda Fletcher during my second trial. While representing her, did he convey any confidential information? Did he know that my version of Fletcher's involvement would not only aid my defense but also bring her up on potential perjury charges? This hearing overturned my conviction, but, of course, allowed the state a timely appeal, which they did with all deliberate speed and fury.

But my hope was growing. I knew I had committed a terrible crime and deserved punishment, but not death. I knew God had planned something better for my life.

CHAPTER 21

Sister Helen Prejean and I corresponded frequently after Karla Faye's death. I noted that at a London conference she said, "Human beings are capable of redemption and change." When people saw and heard Karla Faye Tucker, support for the death penalty dropped to 48 percent in Texas. It is easy to kill a monster but very hard to kill a human being. The people of Texas could see Karla Faye had changed. Yes, she had committed a horrible crime, but over time she had moved beyond that act into a "loving human being."[109] Karla Faye put a face on the death penalty. People could see the love of God shining from her eyes and hear the "unerring faith" in her words.

Where Karla Faye was the poster child for redemption, Betty Lou Beets was a champion for the "mentally ill, the impaired, the abused."[110] These were the factors that influenced her life and subsequently, through her actions, earned her the media nickname: The Black Widow. But she never got a chance to expound on this as fully as I am sure she would have liked, nor on the positive note that she too was redeemed in Christ Jesus. In January 2000, the state scheduled Betty Lou Beets for execution on February 3.

They moved her to the other side from us into a separate cell. With barely thirty days left, she had little time to get help and fight for her life. I know they pushed her execution through quickly so Texas would not have time to see another female face fighting for her life in the media, thereby creating another embarrassment for Governor Bush. Betty Lou had been a member of our family of four—now only three—for fourteen years. I had seen her change from a hardened blonde to a sweet-smiling, sixty-two-year-old great-grandmother with gray hair.

The day room, or rec room as we referred to it, divided our twelve cells in MPF. Both facing sides of Plexiglas allowed me to look and wave at Betty Lou on the other side. In the evening, we would flick our cell lights on and off as a sign of faith for the coming night. When they took me to shower in the morning, the officer let me stop in front of Betty Lou and talk for a few minutes. Prison life has so few pleasures that those it does allow are amplified and treasured. One such simple pleasure is to look out the window and gaze at a tree or a bird. Though it was winter, dark and cloaked in temporary death, Betty Lou could look out her rear windows and absorb God's creations: an evergreen representing life everlasting; the leafless skeleton of a tree, life to be reborn come Easter; and a wren puffed twice her normal size from the cold, the Biblical bird that God knows even when she falls. Then the warden blocked her outside window with a vinyl cover so she couldn't enjoy such a pleasure, a minor thing to many but everything to an inmate. Why they denied her this simple joy in her last moments, I will never understand. It was utterly cruel.

Betty Lou had been abused—physically and mentally—by her former husbands, whom she claimed abused her in part because of her hearing loss. She often quoted Helen Keller on which handicap Helen would have had restored if it could have been. "Hearing," she said, "because hearing connects you with the world." Betty Lou stressed her abuse, her handicap, and her redemption in several publications on the CCADP website and in various media interviews.

Mary Robinson, who was doing a lot of legal work on Betty Lou's case, had T-shirts made with a picture of Betty Lou sporting a black eye from spousal abuse. Mary Robinson held a rally in front of the state capitol in Austin, protesting Betty Lou's execution. I wrote an article to CCADP noting Betty Lou's abuse, that she had brain damage from frequent blows to the head, and that she lost her hearing as a child from measles. I always felt that her head injuries also contributed to her hearing loss. Her attorneys made a last-minute appeal to the Fifth Circuit Court of Appeals and subsequently to the U.S. Supreme Court based upon inept counsel during trial and the fact that her abuse, a mitigating factor, was not introduced in evidence. The court rejected her appeals. The final decision now rested with the Texas Board of Pardons and Paroles.[111, 112]

The Board of Pardons and Paroles voted not to commute Betty Lou's sentence to life nor to grant a 180-day reprieve to review her case. The hoped-for reprieve would have occurred under the 1991 Texas Senate Concurrent Resolution 26 that requires the board to focus upon pardon applicants whose crime arguably was a response to "severe spousal abuse."[113] Since the Board had voted not to consider Resolution 26, Betty Lou's attorneys sued the board, an appeal also rejected by the Fifth Circuit Court. This rejection left little legal option for Governor Bush except to grant a thirty-day stay of execution. He declined and sided with his appointees. The court now rescheduled Betty Lou's execution for February 24. On the eve before, she wrote a farewell letter to her friends that appeared in CCADP.[114]

Dear Friends,

Today has started without me as a part of the human race. I now rest in the arms of My Heavenly Father inside his pearly gates.

Oh, how blessed I was to have you, how blessed I hope I've been to you, to try to show that His grace is all we really need. I never could have made it without our Father's love, without all your love and support. What our Father has brought together let no one tear apart.

My prayer is I've left this hard lesson. Heal the lost, impaired, disabled, battered, and for all who are in need, stick by the banner and carry it on. Help one another right where you are, near or far. Give your heart in all that is right and good. Bring knowledge to those who don't understand, that they can reach out and learn what they can do for themselves and others.

Always remember the battle is not over, but show up, put on the armor of God and let Him fight the battles through us. Then and only then will we win.

Trust that we all ran a good race and we won together. I'll leave this earth knowing I was loved by many. God is pleased and blessed that your faith was instilled in Him. His rewards are yours.

I love you all and will see you on the other side. God blesses you all. Keep the faith and give all the glory to God.

Love,

Betty

* * *

Compared to Karla Faye's execution, Betty Lou's had much less publicity and many fewer protests. There were not very many at a protest rally in Austin and not very many outside Huntsville during her ordeal.

During an execution, beginning at five in the afternoon, an open-chapel service is held at Mountain View for the victim. Executions take place at six, and after the announcement of their being "officially dead," the service concludes. Other than the open-chapel service for Betty Lou, there wasn't much happening that day. I think a part of the nonchalance was due to the fact that Texas had now become inured to killing a female—no big deal.

Jim Willett was the warden at the Walls Unit and presided over Betty Lou's execution. His remarks summarize the public viewpoint as well as that here at Mountain View.

"When Betty Beets' execution was approaching, I worried for my staff and myself as I knew how the execution of Karla Faye Tucker had affected some of the staff. However, Beets did not have much to say and did not exhibit a personality that drew people to her, and it turned out to be no different really than the men I'd dealt with."[115]

Willett and those wardens before and after him are *not* the proverbial ax-wielding executioners in black hoods. They undoubtedly have the most difficult job on this earth. Jim is a Christian with a strong faith who believes in the Biblical principle that the state has the divine right to execute: "…But if you do wrong, be afraid, for he [the state] does not bear the sword for nothing. He [the state] is God's servant, an agent of wrath to bring punishment on the wrongdoer."[116] Note that this is from the New Testament, not the Old that contains the eye-for-an-eye law. Note further that Romans 13:4 is not a mandate; God's mercy on those who have committed murder is biblically well-documented.

For a better understanding of God's heart regarding capital punishment, one should read *The Biblical Truth About America's Death Penalty* by Dale S. Recinella.[117] Recinella received a master's in theological studies from the Ave Maria University Institute of Pastoral Theology and a law degree from the University of Notre Dame. He has taught international law and business ethics in Europe, at St. John's University in Rome and at Temple University in Rome. He is a licensed lawyer in Florida and a prison minister comforting the condemned and their victims. He has published numerous books and articles helping so many to understand God's Word on the death penalty.

Similar to what I had planned for my execution, Betty Lou chose just two witnesses. She solicited her attorney, Joseph Margulies, who had fought to the end for clemency. His remarks after the execution concerning Governor Bush's lack of intervention regarding Margulies' clemency request[118] were anything but complimentary.[119]

Margulies is a well-known attorney with considerable experience in alien-detention law. He is currently "a Visiting Professor of Law and Government at Cornell University…Counsel of Record in *Rasul v. Bush* [then President Bush] (2004), involving detentions at the Guantánamo Bay Naval Station…[and has] written two books…"[120]

For her second witness, Betty Lou chose her pastor, Dr. Paul Carlin, whom she met during his prison ministry.[121] Betty Lou declined her last meal and did not give a last statement. Reports state that she smiled before her final moments.[122]

* * *

Margulies gives a far different account of Betty Lou's execution than that found in the media. Proponents for the death penalty, and those whose feelings are neutral, should read his publication, "The Execution of Betty Lou Beets," Reprieve.org.uk.[123] In that article, Margulies dispels the ancient cliché-myth published by reporters who witness executions with such words, as he points out, as "coughing twice and lapsing into unconsciousness." For whom do they print such euphonic prose? Is it for those with some sensitivity for the gift of life, those who pray silently for the soul of the condemned? Or perhaps, and more likely, as a cynical taunt for those with vengeful hearts, those who would rather read about the condemned thrashing and screaming in agony for an hour.

Margulies points out that Betty Lou, who was barely over five feet in height, was strapped to a large, man-sized, Procrustean gurney, the straps of which he assumed were to prevent her small form from falling to the floor as she fell *gently* to sleep. In reality, he noted that the straps kept her from lurching off the gurney onto the floor, violently in a death-throe agony, during her last breath. Not the *gentle cough* the media would have us believe. And no, she was not smiling when she died. She was smiling at Dr. Carlin and Margulies, whom she could see, *before* that final cough.

"A line of spittle flew out of her mouth and landed on her chin. Her eyes opened wide like discs, and she looked terrified, as though someone had struck her violently from behind, and she knew in that instant that she would die…she gasped, grimacing, trying to draw in the air that had just shot from her body…her eyes closed, and never opened again."[124]

Dr. Carlin[125] was the other witness. In addition to his prison ministry, he is pastor of Shady Grove Baptist Church in Crockett, Texas. His wife, Jeri, taught Sunday school, and through her various meetings with Betty Lou, she joined their church by proxy. They always had an empty chair with her name on it during their meetings. Jeri sent Betty Lou the lessons each month along with the study questions. Betty Lou always returned her answers.

Dr. Carlin said Betty Lou "showed great remorse for her crimes. She deeply regretted her failure as a mother. Before her execution, she asked Jeri and me to find her daughter whom she had not heard from in ten years. She wanted desperately to reconcile with her daughter. After tireless searching, we did finally locate her. Ironically, she was a TDCJ prisoner incarcerated right across the street from Mountain View prison where Betty was. The system arranged for them to visit just prior to her execution date."

Dr. Carlin gives a much more peaceful description of Betty Lou's final journey. "I was there for her execution, visited with her before in her waiting cell, prayed with her, and left her in both of our grief. It was sad. I can say that Betty died quietly. However, the effect it had on me to witness her execution cannot be put into words. It affected me emotionally like nothing ever had before or has since. It is not something I would ever like to do again. We did arrange for her funeral. We did meet with her family at the graveyard, conducted a brief service, and spread her ashes over the grave of (I believe) her mother. It was not the type of funeral a pastor enjoys. Comforting a family in these circumstances is never easy. Betty had made a clear profession in faith in the Lord Jesus Christ. She did give evidence of her peace with God."[126]

* * *

Betty Lou never admitted to any of us on Death Row that she murdered either of her husbands. This fact (that she never admitted her guilt), I understand, was primarily responsible for the board not considering giving her any reprieve or clemency. To get to know Betty Lou was difficult. As I have said before, she didn't trust women. I would have to classify her as a hermit. When Mike Barber or Bill Glass in their prison ministries came and talked with us, Betty Lou came out of her cell, participated in our activities, and was friendly and a joy to our little family. But as soon as they left, she returned to her cell and did not talk to anyone. As sometimes happens to every person when they meet another, an invisible curtain falls between them, a curtain of dislike, a curtain of avoidance—an unexplainable fabric of mutual hostility. This barrier was, in part, instrumental to the strange relationship between Betty Lou and me, one of instant dislike. The other part was that in any time of trouble, we turned to each other. When her mother and son died, both in the same year, Betty Lou lamented to me.

I received a letter from her three days after her execution that she wrote during her I-am-about-to-die preparation in the Goree Unit. She told me that if I had to go through this, the people there were very nice. They put a television outside her cell so she could watch her soap operas. They gave her makeup. The director of TDCJ came and visited her just as he had done for Karla Faye, and he was very nice. It was rather strange receiving a letter from her just after she was no longer with us, and remarkable that she would write to *me* at that point in time. But looking back, that was typical of our unusual relationship. I know that one day, Betty Lou, Karla Faye, and I will all be together and celebrate the unfathomable love of our Father. That earthly rag of a curtain between Betty Lou and me will be no more. This I know. This I believe. This I affirm.

CHAPTER 22

I vaguely remember a country-and-western song about December being the "coldest time of year."[(127)] It came out in mid-1970, but that was during my continuous high—the bottom of my life—so I don't remember all the words. In Texas, however, the coldest time of year is usually in January and February, and it is a different cold, often described as having the North wind separated from the North Pole by a single strand of barbed-wire fence somewhere in the Texas Panhandle. A damp cold, a dreary-gray sky outside that amplifies the dreary-gray concrete inside—the *coldest time of year*. February, a gloomy end to being without Betty Lou every day. With Karla Faye also gone, it was a double shot of angst.

Then March came. March, as the adage says, comes in like a lion and goes out like a lamb. Again, not true in Texas. March *does* come in like a lion with gusty winds that roar all day. But she doesn't bleat lamb-like into April; no, she continues to howl sometimes all the way into May. And her breath may be warm or freezing. As I have always said, compared to California, Texas is a foreign country. Even the weather is foreign. Looking through my window, the outside world came through a fist-wide thickness of Plexiglas, as if looking at freedom from inside a fishbowl. On the second of March, I could see the effects of the lion, evergreen trees afar off bending from side to side like fat old ladies doing aerobics in double time. I could almost feel it coming through the cracks, but there weren't any cracks, just a solid barrier to a distant land.

And also on the second of March, a guard came to my cell and said I had a call from my attorney. She frisked me, handcuffed me, and took me to an office there on Death Row. All five of my attorneys from Baker Botts were on speakerphone. One spoke, "Pam, you might want to sit down before we tell you this."

I said, "I am too nervous to sit down."

"The state has lost all of their appeals. The U.S. Fifth Circuit has affirmed your petition for relief. Their decision upholds a lower-court ruling that the State of Texas, within 120 days, must either retry you or set you free."

No one can imagine the elation, the gratitude to God, the emotional relief of the possibility that I may soon be free from this poisonous snake whose mouth had gaped open for twenty years with fangs poised over the vein in my forearm! That constant threat of impending death in itself should be considered a violation of the Eighth Amendment prohibition of "cruel and unusual punishment." However, several weeks passed while the Texas attorney general's office decided whether to appeal this last ruling. For whatever reason, they chose not to pursue it. A plea bargain was on the table, and two officers drove me to Houston.

Like a kite without a tail, our patrol car flopped from side to side with a growl from the March lion. As usual, whenever I made this trip, I noticed how the world outside was growing: more cars with different shapes and flashy colors, colors like bright purple and chartreuse with sparkling speckles; more new buildings growing ever taller; more people; and more people dressed in different styles. The world outside was growing while mine inside was rather stagnant. Oh, there were some changes if one considered removing certain simple pleasures, but not like changes on the outside. And there was growth in prison if one considered more prisoners and more buildings, but not like the outside. Freedom versus prison is so precious, freedom that no child should ever want to trade for a drug euphoria.

As we departed from the patrol car in the garage under the Houston County Jail, a gust of March wind bowled through the brick-lined alleys into the parking entrance and forced the pungent smell of exhaust into my lungs, a smell long forgotten. Up the familiar back elevator and into the fluorescent midday sunshine of the 248th District Court where soon the bailiff chanted, "All rise. The Honorable Judge Joan Campbell presiding…"

For reasons unknown, the court had appointed me two more attorneys although I still had the five *pro bono* attorneys from Baker Botts. The district attorney then offered me a choice: a plea bargain for life imprisonment or a retrial. It was not a simple *Oh, I'll take door number one for life.* There was a chance that on retrial, I might get a lesser sentence. I asked, "Your Honor, could I think it over?" She let us use an office room downstairs in the basement.

In addition to my five Baker Botts attorneys and two court-appointed attorneys, also present were Mike Barber of Mike Barber Ministries and his wife, DeAnne; my adopted mom, Christina; and my son, Joseph. It was not a conference room, so some of us had to stand. One could almost smell old legal discussions where the fate of one lay in the wisdom of others. One of the attorneys from Baker Botts opened:

"Pam, allow me to go over the details of a meeting we had with people from the district attorney's office. They feel that all the support you have, like Mike Barber Ministries, and your good behavior for twenty years in prison weigh heavily in your favor. The case is old, and there is little chance they can get Linda Fletcher out of California to testify in a new trial, plus her prior testimony was tainted. All of that, along with the addition of mitigating circumstances regarding the death penalty, could preclude a death sentence. Therefore they have offered you a plea bargain.

"These are the details: The two capital murders would be dropped down to two aggravated robberies. The sentence would be life on one of these and thirty years on the other. The sentences would be concurrent."

I responded, "You are saying that my sentences would be stacked? Then what about the twenty years I have already been in prison? What about parole?"

The attorney answered, "The twenty years you have served counts as eligibility for the life sentence. After another ten years, you will be eligible for a full parole."

Mike Barber responded, "Pam, I think you should turn down the plea bargain. As I understand it, the chances are good that you could get a lot less time."

"No, Pam," said Christina, "I would not recommend another trial."

Then my son said, "Mom, please don't take a chance at a trial again and possibly getting the death penalty."

With his humble request, and the pleading look in his eyes that I shall never forget, all I had to do was reflect for a microsecond on how swift my first trial had been, and how quickly they sentenced me to death without any witnesses. Death, based upon nothing but my sincere, conscience-cleansing confession. I decided to go with the plea bargain. I think Mike was upset with my decision, but I felt and still feel that it was the best choice.

The next day, Judge Campbell formally asked me if I had made a decision regarding the plea bargain. After my answer in the affirmative and to the affirmative, Judge Campbell read a summary of the plea bargain and sentenced me to life and thirty years concurrently. But it was not *life without parole*, a somewhat new concept gaining popularity in Texas compared to the death penalty. It was a blurry event, mechanical voices from far off. Back in my cell, the fog lifted, and I knew that Karla Faye, Betty Lou, and the angels were singing in heaven. My heart joined them silently.

I was in the Houston County Jail for several more days while the wheels of paper moved slowly. Needless to state, my emotions were high. I guess one of the guards sensed this, and he offered me a cigarette. About five years had passed since the smoking ban appeared in the prison system. At the time, a cigarette sounded like a good idea. After one puff, I got dizzy, nauseated, and almost threw up. Even the smell of it was making me sick. Surely another drag would be better. It wasn't, and that was the last of any cigarette that I hope and pray I will ever try again.

* * *

A quick return to the general population at Mountain View? No, a change in a prisoner's status takes paperwork, legal stampings, red tape, and time. Lots of time. Even exoneration for a false conviction does not guarantee immediate, on-the-spot release of the inmate. In those instances, the State of Texas reminds me of a dog returning a fetched ball, and when you say, "Drop it," he looks at you with some sort of deep grin in his eyes until you pry it out of his mouth.

The Texas penal system refers to my "in limbo" status as being *in transit*, and the inmate, a *transient*. They kept me in the high-profile tank in Houston for about a week, the same high-profile tank where I had been when I met Karla. Then I moved to the Plane State Jail.

The Plane State Jail[128] was founded in 1995. There is no town named Plane, Texas; the facility was named for Lucile Plane,[129] the former warden of Mountain View. Plane State is a small women's prison housing low-level offenders and transients such as me, the ball in the dog's mouth as he runs about, refusing to bring it home. It was only a forty-five minute drive to the Plane State Jail in Dayton, northeast of Houston. Immediately, I went into Ad Seg, separated from the general population because of my *high-profile* status. I was there for a week, primarily to get a new number; my old number, 665, was an execution number. My new number, 932235, became the one I would bear for years to come.

After I received my new number, I journeyed to the Goree Unit in Huntsville, again as a transient, entering their diagnostic unit for evaluation and classification. As noted earlier, all female prisoners, including myself, were transferred from Goree to Mountain View in 1981 when Goree converted into a male prison unit. However, it still is used for female transients. After several weeks there, I entered the Reception

Center at the Crain Unit. For forty-five days, I was still *in transit*. This status might as well be synonymous with *incognito*: No one knows where you are or how to contact you.

Christina and Joseph had frantically called almost every telephone number for TDCJ trying to find me, but to no avail. Finally, the warden at the Hilltop Unit,[130] also located in Gatesville, agreed to take me. Looking back, it was as if no one wanted me since I wasn't dead.

Hilltop started out wonderfully. The unit is a small facility for female youth offenders, housing probably no more than 400 inmates at that time. I was there as a youth offender counselor and was enjoying my purpose in life.

CHAPTER 23

The greener grass on that side of the fence turned brown overnight. I discovered that one who "cheats the hangman" is open to scorn from both officers and inmates. I had received the mark of Cain:[131] they would not kill me, but they would shun me. Whenever I was coming to or from work across the yard, along the main street of the Hilltop Unit, there was always a group of guards, a group of inmates, or a mixed group of guards with inmates pointing at me and talking. One conversation between two guards spoken just a few feet from me was most memorable, and they did not try to hide it.

"I did some figuring the other day, and do you know that all of the tax money we've spent to keep her on Death Row would have put our children through college?"

"Yeah," said the other, "she did beat the system."

"No doubt about it, they should have executed her."

My "house" was always in shambles when I returned to it from wherever I'd been, my belongings scattered on the bed and floor. Even the faceplate for the electrical outlet was often unattached. Invariably, my radio was missing, and I had to go to the property room and beg it back. On many occasions while I was walking on Main Street, a guard would commandeer me into a shower and subject me to a strip search.

One of the sergeants at the Hilltop Unit was always on my back, making snide remarks and giving me frequent pat-downs—constantly in my face, as they say—another of those self-appointed justice dealers, but far more persistent.

Then it happened. A Texas-hot, mid-summer sun raised my bubbling point to bursting one afternoon. I am convinced the sun in Texas dips down from its arc over the globe by a few million miles, but then, if the winters are that of a foreign country, then why shouldn't the summers be also. I walked up to the sergeant on Main Street and asked, "Do you have a political view that you want to talk to me about?"

"Well, that depends. Are you a Republican or are you a Democrat?"

"Whatever my political beliefs are do not matter, but what does matter is the State of Texas decided that I should get off Death Row. Now if you have a problem with that, then you should take it up with the State of Texas."

He made some smart remark and turned away. After that, he kind of backed off a little, but not much. He was also one of the guards that I had complained to Warden Nancy Botkin about. Maybe she had spoken to him. But overall, the persecution continued, so I again complained to Warden Botkin, who called me into her office.

"Warden, I am so tired of constantly being harassed. Can't you do something?"

"Pam, it's because your case received so much attention and that you are what we call 'high-profile.' Eventually, it will die down. These things always do."

And it did, maybe by the width of a hair. Then in late autumn, what once looked like green grass turned brown and bitter. It was a Saturday. That morning, Christina and Joseph had visited me. Around eleven that night, I was sitting in the day room watching TV when two officers approached. One was a high rank, maybe a sergeant or a lieutenant.

"Ms. Perillo, would you step out in the hallway?" When I did, they handcuffed me and took me to Ad Seg.

"What is this for? Why are you taking me there?"

No answers, and their frowns said as little as their silence. With no sheets for my mattress, not even toilet tissue, I waited in that cell until Sunday morning when they escorted me to Major Henson's office. When I entered, I looked with awe at everything I owned—what little there was— scattered and open all over her carpet, in front of her desk, to the sides, everywhere a tornado could have dropped them. Everyone was standing when I entered, including a man in a suit who asked me to step into an adjoining office. Without any introduction, he said, "Sit down. Did you have a visit with your mom and son Saturday, yesterday morning?"

"Yes, sir," I replied.

"Did you discuss the escape?"

"Escape? What escape? What are you talking about?"

"Just answer my question. Did you discuss the escape?"

"Sir, I'm sorry, I don't know what you are talking about."

"We received two anonymous telephone calls yesterday," he paused and glared, "that your adopted mom and your son were going to break you out of prison at twelve o'clock that night. You do know about this?"

"That's ridiculous."

"Just answer my question. Did you discuss the escape?"

"No, that's ridiculous. Why would she risk a high-paying career, and why would my son risk his future when he is about to graduate from Texas A&M? Why would they risk their lives to break me out of prison and go on the run with me? Especially since I have just gotten off Death Row and will be eligible for parole. I would never ask them to do something like that. If they were ever going to attempt something that stupid, why didn't they do it when I was two days away from execution? Not now. That doesn't make any sense. That doesn't make even good nonsense."

I was screaming at this point and he kept yelling back, "Just answer the question! Did you discuss the escape?" The interrogation pretty much ended, and they took me back to the lockup in Ad Seg.

Warden Botkin called me into her office two hours later and said, "Pam, just calm down. I'm sure this is all some bizarre mistake, maybe some kind of a joke, but we do have to take these things seriously. We will be making an investigation, and as soon as that is complete, I am sure you will be able to come back up [out of Ad Seg]."

"Warden, I don't know who is making these phone calls, but whoever it is knows that I have a mom and a son. Maybe it's one of the officers or maybe it's someone on the outside who is mad because I got off Death Row. But they do know I have a mom and a son. I don't understand…"

"Well, whoever it was, we know that it was a female, and we did hear children in the background."

"It's absolutely ridiculous. Why would my family give up their lives to do something like that?"

"Don't worry about it, Pam. It will all work out."

On Tuesday, they packaged me up and moved me from Hilltop into the Mountain View Unit and into their Ad Seg. Printed on the card outside my cell: "Transient Pending Investigation." For ten days, I could not see my family, no one. And Warden Page of the Mountain View Unit kept telling my family and me that everything would be all right. Finally, Christina reached her ignition point and called the Warden early that Friday.

"This is preposterous. You haven't even questioned her son or me in this matter. You either charge her or let her up from Ad Seg, or you can expect a lawsuit on your desk Monday morning."

At five o'clock that evening, they released me into the general population—no comments, no explanation. I have never heard another word about the *Great Escape,* nor has any of my family.

About a month later, the mark of Cain appeared again. My supervisor, several others, and I were painting the walls of the visiting room. The door was locked. When a pair of handheld garden shears turned up missing from a crew working outside, the unit went into a lockdown that continued for four days. During this period, the warden called me into her office and said, "Because of the incident at Hilltop, did you take the hand clippers and were you going to try to use them to get out?"

"Come on," I said. "Now, what would I do with a pair of hand clippers? Where would I go with them?"

"I know it sounds crazy, Pam, but I have to ask you this question because of what you recently went through over at Hilltop."

"No, ma'am, I did not take the hand clippers," and a few days later, they found the clippers where the yard girl had left them. For several years, when something went wrong it was *pick on Pam; she must have done it.*

CHAPTER 24

In addition to constant harassment in my new environment, I endured another type of unexpected adjustment: noise. Whereas I had been in a private cell with a few other inmates on Death Row, I was now housed in a dormitory with thirty-four other women. We each had an open-top cubicle containing a bed with a table attached to it. It was frightening. I couldn't sleep with all these other people around me. For almost twenty years, I had been more or less alone. A background roar rumbled through the partitions nonstop, day and night, 24/7. Not the soothing sound such as that from a fan or air conditioner, no sleep-inducing hum; no, this motor had a huge megaphone attached that randomly blared out screams and yells, pleas for mercy, and most frequently, curse words. A women's prison dorm is a different sort of village.

* * *

By 2004, the State of Texas tightened its coils in preparation to strike Frances Elaine Newton, the last of the three who began Death Row with me. The Texas Board of Pardons and Parole recommended their customary 120-day stay of execution to Governor Rick Perry, who on the next day signed the executive order for the stay. This reprieve stressed the need for an additional ballistic analysis on the alleged murder weapon and a review of the nitrates (gunshot residue or fertilizer) on the hem of Frances' skirt. The first question, which still remains to date: Why did police wait two weeks to arrest Frances when the second day after the murder the Houston Police Department Crime Lab had confirmed that the gun hidden in Frances' blue bag was indeed the murder weapon? Most feel that Sgt. J.J. Freeze's testimony stating that he heard of a second gun might have been responsible. Sgt. Freeze also told Frances' father that they would release Frances because the ballistic test did not implicate her. The second gun (never recovered), coupled with Sgt. Freeze's refusal to talk to counsel for Frances, still leaves a dark cloud over this one of two pieces of circumstantial evidence.

On the other piece of "evidence," the state originally used a destructive test to determine nitrates *per se*, thereby preventing the defense from using a test that would differentiate between gunshot residue and fertilizer. It was noted that Frances' daughter had contact with fertilizer from her uncle's garden and could have transferred the nitrates to the hem of Frances' dress—certainly consistent with the hugging action of a twenty-one-month-old girl. As also noted earlier, Frances would have had to have shot her family with her hands on the floor. Procedures were available at that time to make a differential in nitrates, but HPD decided not to use them. They also placed the skirt in the same evidence box with the victims' clothing, thus introducing cross-contamination.

The stay of execution for Frances was only that, a paper stay. An execution date was set for September 14, 2005. A writ of *habeas corpus* and a motion for a stay of execution were then filed in the 263rd Judicial District Court of Harris County in May 2005 and subsequently denied.

Two days before Frances' scheduled execution, the Texas Board of Pardons[132] voted 7–0 to deny her request for a commutation to life imprisonment. Like Betty Lou Beets, Frances made no final statement and refused a request for a last meal. I understand that to the end, Frances expected to receive clemency. There is no doubt in my mind that she was innocent. Those who oppose the death penalty do so for many reasons. The first and primary reason was embodied in Frances Newton: murdering the innocent. I did not get to see Frances before she left. Warden Baggett was no longer there, and the new warden, Nance, would not allow me to visit her.

On the day they executed Frances, I was working in maintenance, the day's task consisting of digging a large hole because of a broken water pipe. Early September is still summer in Texas; fall doesn't start until months later and is a brief respite at best. The temperature reached the mid-nineties that afternoon. When I got off work at four, I returned to my dorm. After a shower, I just lay on my bed and prayed. I did not eat dinner. I did not listen to the news. I did not want to hear about Frances' passing. At the customary 6 p.m. deadline, they injected the poison. I am sure the media reported that she coughed once, closed her eyes, and died peacefully, but that is their interpretation. No one knows how peaceful it was. I'll ask Frances when I see her again.

Shortly after 6 p.m. that September 14, 2005, Warden Nance and Chaplain Nelson came to the dorm and asked me to step outside. Chaplain Nelson did most of the talking: "Pamela, we stopped by to let you know that the execution went as planned. I am sure she now rests in the arms of Jesus. We felt it better to let you know this personally rather than hear it from another source." I thanked them. It helped.

I understand that there were the usual for-and-against protests in Huntsville but with a much, much smaller crowd than that for Karla Faye. Executing women had now become a sort of ho-hum affair as the State of Texas "pharoahed" its heart to become super tough on crime. It was just the same as any other day in the general population. Few of the inmates even knew who Frances Newton was. But I knew her, and I anguished over why God had taken Karla Faye, Betty Lou, and now Frances instead of me. She was the third female executed since the Civil War and the third of those who had been with me for almost twenty years on Death Row. Who will take joy in her sweet gentle spirit? Maybe that is why God took her home to be with Him.

This handwritten note was on the back of her picture, below, in flowing script:

Frances Elaine McLemore Newton

To Pam:

God has a purpose for us all; sometimes that purpose is not revealed to us. Even so, we have to press on and glorify Him each day. Some days are harder than others, but I know that if we keep our focus on Him, He will sustain us in all of our ways.

Running for Jesus,

Frances

At the end of 2009, I applied for the Faith-Based Dorm program. The Faith-Based Dorm was the inspiration of Karla Faye Tucker. She had a dream whereby inmates could come together and share the love of Jesus in a separate dormitory. The dorm was reserved not for just those who had found Christ, but also for those who were searching. The chaplain at Mountain View asked Linda Strom[133] to head this newly created program. I interviewed with Linda in the Chapel of Hope and within a week moved into the program.

The Faith-Based Dorm program lasts eighteen months. At the end of the program, there is a graduation ceremony and a certificate of completion. It is an excellent program. The dorm is similar in layout to the general-population dorms. There are cubicles for fifty-six inmates. They follow the same rules and regulations, except there is a mandatory quiet time from noon to 2 p.m. Everyone returns to their cubicle and there is no talking, no music playing, just silence—the only location on the whole compound where there is ever pure peace and quiet. It is such a blessing. One may pray, read her Bible, or meditate in "...the peace of God, which passeth all understanding..."[134] In the evening, one of the inmates gives a devotional. The devotional leader moves daily from bed number one to the next bed in line until all fifty-six have ministered, and then it begins anew. The devotional lasts from fifteen to twenty minutes, and the person may give a testimony, read from the Bible, or share a faith-based moment in her life. On Monday, Tuesday, Thursday, and Saturday, volunteers from the outside present Bible studies such as those from Dr. Henry Blackaby[135] and videos from Dr. David Jeremiah.[136]

On Sundays, two services are held in the chapel, morning and evening, with mandatory attendance. When you graduate, you have a firm foundation in Christ, good Biblical knowledge, and meaningful fellowship with others. Further information appears in a live interview by CBN.[137] If you look closely, you can see me in several frames.

Also, note the two remarkable things that glisten in this video: the spirit-filled eyes of the believers and the perspiration on their faces. The Faith-Based Dorm, like that of the general population, is not air-conditioned.

God speaks to us. He speaks to us in a jillion different ways: directly, such as in the Garden of Eden, to appearing in dreams to Joseph, both of these in the Old Testament. And in the New Testament, in a blinding vision to Saul of Tarsus on the road to Damascus.[138] God speaks to each of us differently according to the makeup of our soul and according to our needs. One of His ways that I treasure most is through dreams. One knows when a dream is from God because it is *not* the average snippet, the little pieces of anxiety or old memories we receive every so often. And though such mundane dreams may seem very real, we know they are but earthly; spiritual dreams are on a much higher plane. They always remain a hundred percent intact in our memory. You immediately know the difference—the lighting is supernatural, the location is somewhere far from dreamland, and the voices penetrate your deepest being to an indescribable extent. This dream is one from God that I will treasure to my last breath:

My dad, who passed away in 1987, and I were in a room where there wasn't any furniture except two straight-backed, wooden chairs. Everything was white—the chairs, the room, everything, a bright white, an indescribable white—white that was transparent with every color and shade hidden within, a white that was shiny and haloed, a white that only God could create. Dad told me that he loved me, and I told him that I loved him also. He asked for my forgiveness, which I readily offered. Then we hugged each other, and I could feel the tears on both our faces. As our contact faded, I awoke. I have never experienced such joy and peace.

* * *

After I graduated from the Faith-Based program, I entered the service dog program. The program is called Patriot PAWS Service Dogs and is based in Rockwall, Texas, just east across Lake Ray Hubbard from Dallas.[139] In addition to their many other trainers, inmates from the Lane Murray Unit in Gatesville also train service dogs. The dogs assist disabled American veterans and others with physical and emotional disabilities, such as those who have lost limbs and those who suffer post-traumatic stress disorder (PTSD) and traumatic brain injury (TBI). For the physically disabled, we teach the dogs to get emergency help, retrieve items, open and close doors, and even pull a wheelchair. For PTSD and TBI, what better service could a dog provide than being man's best friend? When the dogs graduate from the inmate-training program, they are presented to the veteran, usually in a ceremony at the location where the dogs were trained. At this ceremony, the dogs and their new owner choose each other. It is amazing to see how they instinctively match up. And the dogs know the difference between their new owners and us, their trainers. This is obvious by their expressions and response to commands. The emotion shown by these heroes who are missing limbs and hurting, as well as the emotions shown by the trainers—that passion is overwhelming. Neither the trainers nor the veterans ever have dry eyes.

I have always loved animals, and this is my way of giving back to the world from which I took so much. I will always be most grateful to Lori Stevens, the founder and executive director of Patriot Paws, and to all the Rockwall, Texas, trainers for giving me the life-changing opportunity to participate in their program.

I still participate in the Faith-Based Dorm program. I go to their graduations, to the reunions of former graduates, and to the baptisms. I reside in the general-population dorm. There are many other programs for Christians at Mountain View, such as Kairos.

One should interpret *kairos* [140] as God's special time when a person reflects upon the past and the future and his opportunity to know the

Kingdom of God, that special moment during an indeterminate interval in unbounded time when God's salvation enters one's heart and soul.

The Kairos Prison Ministry International, Inc. (KPMI)[141] chose its name appropriately. KPMI provides a four-day "walk" (retreat) for prison inmates. Although we do not get to leave the prison for a walk, we enjoy some home-cooked meals, brought by volunteers, in the rec room. We spend most of the day there and get to hear various talks from the volunteers, sing, participate in activities, and join in discussions; it's just a real love-based program. When you have been in there for four days, you don't even feel like you are locked up; you are in a place where agape love surrounds you in another realm. It is open to all faiths and to those who don't even believe in God. At the conclusion, each inmate may talk about what the program meant to her. Many give themselves to Christ. After the four-day walk, you become a member of Kairos. Every Wednesday night, we go to the chapel and break into groups that are called "Prayer and Share," where we discuss difficult situations in our Christian walk and enjoy fellowship with each other. Kairos also has a three-day walk for those on the outside called "Walk to Emmaus."[142] We also have different Bible study groups. They have services for Jehovah's Witnesses, Native Americans, Catholics, Muslims, Buddhists, and other faiths. They also offer classes such as Anger Management, Support for the Sexually Abused, and many other self-help programs.

* * *

Shortly after I returned to the general-population dorm, I was called into the major's office. Some people from the Discovery Channel wanted to do an interview with another girl and me who had gotten off Death Row. They said it was for their *Faces of Evil* series. I declined. My face and my soul are no longer evil. I later learned that they did the show anyway, Episode 1, Series 60, titled "Hunting Humans," on August 17, 2012.[143] Although I haven't seen it, I have heard that it appears to emphasize non-factual sensationalism—the very reason I have avoided media interviews.

In June 2013, the state executed the third female following Karla Faye Tucker, bringing the total to date at four. Kimberly McCarthy received the dubious honor of being the 500th prisoner executed in Texas since the Supreme Court of the United States reinstated the death penalty in 1976. Kimberly was black, bringing the four women executed at this point to two whites and two blacks.

I remember Kimberly from Death Row. She entered right before I left. She was very sweet and had a precious laugh just like that of a little girl. Those here in Lane Murray, where I live now, did not know her, and most were not even familiar with her case.

I share her last words here so that she may be remembered:

"I just wanted to say thanks to all who have supported me over the years: Reverend Campbell, for my spiritual guidance; Aaron, the father of Darrian, my son; and Maurie, my attorney. Thank you, everybody. This is not a loss; this is a win. You know where I am going. I am going home to be with Jesus. Keep the faith. I love y'all. Thank you, Chaplain."

Kimberly's execution on a Wednesday at 6 p.m. went largely unnoticed in our dorm…in Texas…in the world. The glass ceiling for killing women had been broken.

CHAPTER 26

Every family has a skeleton in its closet. Such a fact is, as they say, "a given." Shh…don't ever tell anyone that Uncle Joe died of cirrhosis from drinking too much, or that Aunt Sue left her husband and became a woman of the street. It happens. And man in his vast wisdom continues to volley this truism between genetics and environment, where genetics corresponds to DNA and environment corresponds to a learned action. The argument is often referred to as nature vs. nurture, respectively. Regardless of which side of the net you choose, God has already spoken on the matter in Exodus 20:5 (KJV), Exodus 34:7 (KJV), Numbers 14:18 (KJV), and Deuteronomy 5:9 (KJV). In these passages, one finds this repeated phrase: "…visiting the iniquity of the fathers upon the children unto the third and fourth generation…"

So what we accept as a fact of life, we learned its cause long before we tried to impart *our* wisdom (genetics or environment). It is note-worthy that God tells us about this several times. As noted earlier in this book, *iniquity* in these passages is often accepted by many theologians[144, 145, 146] as corresponding to an inclination, a propensity, and a tendency. Although these passages lead to considerable religious debate, many feel that we should not interpret the term *iniquity* as sin, per se, nor visit it as a curse upon future generations. There are just too many Biblical passages regarding God's mercy and grace, and that He would not punish the children for the sins of the fathers. Alcoholism or drug abuse in a family, as it passes down from generation to generation, is possibly the clearest example of this iniquity or "human condition." The tendency, whether genetic or environmental, toward addiction is, as noted, already there. When it does become an addiction, then there are problems. And how does one break this pattern? I know, and I am seeing the answer unfold in my family's life.

* * *

The last time I had seen any of my family was during my second trial. From then, I had no contact, just an occasional letter, not even a visit when my father died in 1987.

Randy wrote to me after I was out of Death Row in mid-2012 and came to visit shortly thereafter. We had a wonderful, emotionally charged reunion. He had changed so much from the little boy who took his anger out on innocent animals. Randy had come to Christ through his second wife and was working as a youth minister in California. Both he and his wife take an active part in the ministry for their church. One of his missions is to minister to the youth on the streets. Randy spoke about my father.

"Do you know anything about how Dad died?" he asked.

"No, you're the first contact I have had with any of the family since my second trial—gosh, that's been twenty-something years ago."

"Dad had been fishing and somehow broke his leg."

"How?" I asked.

"I don't know; maybe he twisted it getting out of the boat. But it was pretty bad. He went to the ER where they put pins in it. When they opened his leg, they found bone cancer. It spread fast after that. We took him in at our house and cared for him. Before he went into a coma, he found salvation and asked for our forgiveness, each of us. I know we'll see him again where there will be no pain and suffering. In the end, he was covered in bed sores; I turned him regularly and dried them best I could. He died in my arms, Pam."

Through the film of tears in my eyes, I could see the same pooling in Randy's. It had been a long, arduous journey to this special intersection in time. What a precious gift Randy had brought me: not only had he found salvation, but so had my Dad as well. This news, together with my son, Joseph, being a Christian, made me think my heart would burst. I also heard from Ronnie, who had found salvation and is currently in prison. We still correspond. Whatever *iniquity* had been visited upon the Walker family, God no longer remembered it against these.

As for the rest of my family, I know very little. My biological mother's "pill-popping" and Dad's alcoholism after Mom left had passed down to me and was, as best I know, still with my older sister, Joanne. I don't know where she is, but the last I heard was that she was an alcoholic, and I know she has been married at least nine times. Almost all of her husbands, as I understand, were abusive. Of course, I am quite familiar with the last one I knew of, the ninth one, the one who ran us off the road and caused my premature delivery of twins. Joanne's selection of spouses seems to come from neighborhood bars. I pray that Joanne reaches her personal bottom soon and turns upward toward salvation.

My stepmother, Helen, if she is still living, is in California. My half-sister, Donna, also lives there. My brother David is in prison in Nevada, and my brother Dale, who has never been in trouble, has a child and is living in Oklahoma. I continue to pray for all of my family.

At a certain stage in life, I suppose we all reflect on what we have done and how we wish we had done some things differently. Whether we compare our past to a journey, a book, or a tapestry, there are paths, chapters, and threads that we wish were not there. Mine are ever before me. Like the gray weather that I was born in, I look out every day upon the gray concrete that surrounds me. And I remember. With reflection comes the quest for reason. Why? Was it all because of external problems: a dysfunctional home—I should say a house rather than a home, a small wood box of which I was ashamed; peer pressure, to run with older youngsters and do cool drugs; unloving parents, a mother who abandoned me and a father who molested me? Were drugs the root cause?

Collateral causes for sure, but no, the problems were internal. Me, a child of God, given free will, and, most regretfully, I chose drugs. I committed a brutal crime. During thirty-six years of incarceration, I pray daily for forgiveness from the families I hurt.

Have I paid my dues in prison? Is anyone able to pay on earth for what they do on earth? At least my spiritual dues were paid some 2,000 years ago on Calvary. With God's forgiveness and mercy, I hope to live out my days free from these walls.

In January 2016, I learned from my most recent review that my release had been denied. After thirty-five years in prison, I was disheartened. But most devastating was learning that it will be January 2019 before I receive another review. This will mean, when I get out then—thinking and praying on the positive—that I will have been incarcerated almost thirty-nine years.

When I do get out, the first thing on my list is to join the Calvary Commission Refuge Program[147] near Palestine, Texas. They have a

Christian respite, a transitional program, where I can learn how to function and adjust to a world I haven't seen in over three and a half decades. We are able to notice some changes in the world while in prison. We can touch the electronic age and receive e-mails. We can read magazines and see the new styles. We can read newspapers and follow current events. But no, it can never be the same as being free. Freedom, I want to experience it gradually and under instruction from a Christian perspective.

I want to have a home church and to feel like a normal human being. After that, I would like to continue training dogs for the disabled. Yes, I would still like to do what I am doing now. I feel that this is something for which Providence divinely molded me through life and a means whereby I can give back to the world some of so much I have taken. I know we are all given a purpose, and I joy and rest in knowing mine.

Thank you for reading my story. Thank you for your understanding. Thank you for allowing me to express in writing my thanks to my Savior, to Christina, and to Joseph for my very life. Thank you for your prayers and support.

Lord Bless,
Pam Perillo, 2017

Pamela Lynn Perillo, 2013

ACKNOWLEDGMENTS

Thanks to Pam Perillo for allowing an inexperienced writer to tell her story, a story of encouragement and faith, and special thanks for allowing literary license when her memory was sketchy. Also, thanks to Pam for permitting my innate cynicism to bubble forth on occasion wherein it did not necessarily portray her character.

Thanks to Barbara Thorngren for many hours spent in content editing, correcting misspelled words and malaprops. But mostly, thanks for all of her encouragement to complete this project.

Thanks to Julie Webb, professional freelance editor and proofreader, Ajijic, Jalisco, Mexico, for her microscopic thoroughness in ferreting out a legion of grammatical errors.

Thanks to editor and writer Erin Wood of Little Rock, Arkansas-based Wood Writing and Editing (woodwritingandediting.com) for the final touch of excellence in content revision and proofing.

* * *

A special thanks to the following in first-name alphabetical order for their communications and help:

Andy Horne, former assistant U.S. attorney and an assistant district attorney for Harris County before entering private practice. Andy is now retired and lives in Galveston, Texas, where he enjoys being the noted author of the *Decent Men* series.

Evan Greenspan, owner of Greenspan's, 3405 Tweedy Boulevard, South Gate, CA 90280, est. 1928, "specializing in hard to find classic items from the '30s, '40s, '50s, and '60s."

James (Jim) Willett, former warden of the Walls Unit in Huntsville, Texas, where lethal injections are administered. Jim entered employment with the Texas Department of Criminal Justice while in college at Huntsville. Like many of us in our careers, he stayed in the same place where he felt needed. For three years as the warden, he had the hardest job in America—a job he initially turned down—that of officiating at the execution of those convicted and condemned by the state. Jim is a confessed Christian. To gain an insight into his character, one should read *Warden: Prison Life and Death from the Inside Out*, written by Jim and his close friend, Ron Rozelle. Jim is now director of the Texas Prison Museum in Huntsville.

Joseph Margulies, a visiting professor of law and government at Cornell University and a well-known civil rights proponent.

Linda Strom, author of *Karla Faye Tucker Set Free: Life and Faith on Death Row*, and a prison minister of immense encouragement to all who know her.

Mark White, former attorney general for the State of Texas and then the governor of Texas, for comments on the Ruíz decision. Mark passed away on August 5, 2017, prior to this publication. He will be deeply missed.

Paul Carlin, D.D., pastor of Shady Grove Baptist Church, Crockett, Texas.

* * *

I am indebted to all who allowed me to freely paraphrase or quote from their published works in the interest of journalism.

General References

The Holy Bible, King James Version (KJV), Regency Publishing House, Nashville, Tennessee, 1964.

The Holy Bible, New International Version (NIV), Zondervan Publishing House, Grand Rapids, Michigan, 1984.

Atkins v. Virginia, No. 00-8452 (2002), Supreme Court of the United States.

Betty Lou Beets, Petitioner-appelle, Cross-appellant v. James A. Collins, Director of Criminal Justice, Institutional Division, Respondent-appellant, Cross-appelle, United States Court of Appeals, Fifth Circuit, No. 91-4606. 986F.2d 1478, March 18, 1993.

Briddle v. Caldwell, No. 80SA374 (1981), Supreme Court of Colorado.

Burnett v. State, 754 S.W.2d 437 (1988), Court of Criminal Appeals of Texas, San Antonio.

Burnett v. State, 642S.W.2d 765 (1982), Court of Criminal Appeals of Texas, *en banc.*

David Owen Brooks v. State of Texas (05/16/79), Court of Criminal Appeals of Texas, Harris County.

Frances Elaine Newton, Appellant v. The STATE of Texas, Appelle, 263rd, Judicial District, Harris County, 1992 WL 175742, No. 70770, June 17, 1992.

Frances Elaine Newton, Petitioner-appellant, v. Doug Dretke, Director, Texas Department of Criminal Justice, Correctional Institutions Division, Respondent-appelle, United States Court of Appeals, Fifth Circuit. 371 F.3d 250, May 20, 2004.

Perkinson, Robert, *Texas Tough, The Rise of America's Prison Empire*, Picador, Henry Holt & Company, New York, NY, 2010.

James Michael Briddle, Petitioner-appellant v. Wayne Scott, Director Texas Department of Criminal Justice, Institutional Division, Respondent-appelle, United States Court of Appeals, Fifth Circuit, 63 F.3d 364, Aug 23, 1995.

Karla Faye Tucker, Petitioner-appellant, v. Gary L Johnson, Director of Criminal Justice, Institutional Division, Respondent-appelle, United States Court of Appeals, Fifth Circuit. – 115F.3d 276.

Karla Faye Tucker, Petitioner-appellant, v. Gary L Johnson, Director of Criminal Justice, Institutional Division, Respondent-appelle, United States Court of Appeals, Fifth Circuit. – 115F.3d 276.

Pamela Lynn Perillo vs. State of Texas (09/14/88), Appeal from Harris County.

Pamela Lynn Perillo, Petitioner-appellant v. Gary L. Johnson, Director Texas Department of Criminal Justice, Institutional Division, Respondent-appelle, United States Court of Appeals, Fifth Circuit - 79F.3d 441.

Pamela Lynn Perillo, Petitioner-appellant v. Gary L. Johnson, Director Texas Department of Criminal Justice, Institutional Division, Respondent-appelle, United States Court of Appeals, Fifth Circuit, 205 F.3d 775, March 2, 2000.

Pamela Lynn Perillo, Petitioner-appellant v. Gary L. Johnson, Director Texas Department of Criminal Justice, Institutional Division, Respondent-appelle, United States Court of Appeals, Fifth Circuit – 94-20759, March 21, 1996.

Pamela Lynn Perillo, Petitioner-appellant v. Gary L. Johnson, Director Texas Department of Criminal Justice, Institutional Division, Respondent-appelle, United States Court of Appeals, Fifth Circuit – 98-20653, March 2, 2000.

Penry v. Johnson, No. 00-6677 (2001), Supreme Court of the United States.

Penry v. Lynaugh, No. 87-6177 (1989), Syllabus, Supreme Court of the United States.

Perillo v. State, 656 S.W.2d 78 (1983), No. 68872, Court of Criminal Appeals of Texas.

State Bar of Texas, Criminal Justice Section, The Texas Criminal Justice Process – a Citizen's Guide, July 9, 2012.

Atkins v. Virginia, No. 00-8452 (2002), Supreme Court of the United States.

Karla Faye Tucker, Petitioner-appellant, v. Gary L Johnson, Director of Criminal Justice, Institutional Division, Respondent-appelle, United States Court of Appeals, Fifth Circuit. – 115F.3d 276.

LET THE RECORD SHOW
JANE WAS HANGED FIRST
The Dallas Morning News

Date: December 13, 1987

Column: "KENT BIFFLE'S TEXANA"

Author: Kent Biffle

Edition: HOME FINAL

Section: TEXAS & SOUTHWEST

Page: 41A

Reprinted by request and with permission of *The Dallas Morning News*

Chipita, move over.

Generations of Texans have grown up believing that Chipita Rodriguez, a convicted killer who was launched into legend from a South Texas tree limb on November 13, 1863, was the only woman legally hanged in Texas. No way, Jose.

A decade before Chipita was executed in San Patricio County, a woman was legally hanged in Dallas County. The murderer convicted by Dallas County jurors was a slave named Jane, sometimes called Jane Elkins. Today she is a dim, distant figure. But that she hanged is a fact.

Texas history books often give Chipita a solitary distinction she didn't want or deserve. For example, in 1970, Vernon Smylie of Corpus Christi wrote *A Noose for Chipita*. The book's cover proclaims: "The strange case of the only woman ever legally hanged in Texas."

An entry on Chipita in the *Handbook of Texas*, compiled by the Texas State Historical Association, begins:

"Chipita Rodriguez was the only woman ever legally hanged in Texas. Chipita (possibly a misspelling of Chepita, a diminutive of Chepa, nickname for Josefa) lived in a hut at a way station for travelers on the Welder ranch lands on the Aransas River on a trail that led from adjoining Refugio County down to the Rio Grande and Mexico. San Patricio County records show that in August 1863, she along with Juan Silvera (Juan "Chiquito") was accused of the murder of an unknown man whose body was found in the Aransas River near Chipita's cabin. Later accounts call the man John Savage, a horse trader on his way to Mexico carrying gold...Debunking the Bible."

The *Handbook*, a reference bible for Texas historians, is now being revised and enlarged for the 1990s by historical association researchers and editors under the direction of Ron Tyler, an able historian. Tyler, in the new edition, should accord Dallas County its long overdue recognition as a community of woman hanger

Incidentally, Texas hasn't claimed a woman's life since the state began performing all executions at Huntsville in 1924.

Through the years, Jane has been ignored while Chipita has captured much attention in newspapers, magazines and books. Chipita's hanging inspired a piece in *Old West* magazine headlined "The Curse That Killed San Patricio Town." Something cursed that town. Once an important commercial center and county seat, it's a dot on today's map. Sinton is now the county seat.

Chipita's ghost haunts the Nueces River banks where the hanging tree stood. Or so wrote Marylyn Underwood in a popular 1981 book, *Legendary Ladies of Texas.*

One cannot blame Chipita—who denied the murder charge—for being restless. If she didn't get a bum rap, she got a bum trial.

The whole case was circumstantial. Moreover, the sheriff, who arrested her, served as foreman of the grand jury that indicted her. Apparently, three of the grand jurors served on the trial jury.

Four members of the grand jury and trial jury had faced felony indictments shortly before dealing with Chipita. Apparently, six of the grand jurors were employed by the county or had lawsuits pending before the trial judge. And the prosecutor had been under two indictments that were dropped before Chipita's trial.

At least it was swift. Two days after the fall term of court began in 1863, Chipita was indicted.

Two days after that, she was convicted. The following day she was sentenced to die 34 days later, a Friday the 13th. Chipita's attorney withdrew a motion for a new trial. And the judge ignored the jury's recommendation of mercy. The recommendation stemmed from her advanced years. Her exact age isn't known.

John Silvera, who was 50, was convicted of second-degree murder and sentenced to five years in prison.

Although universally forgotten outside Dallas, Jane's case is familiar to some local history buffs and courthouse staffers. For example, Sheriff's Detective June Gunn, Deputy Nancy Stout, retired Deputy O'Byrne Cox and Donald Payton of the Dallas County Historical Society told me what they knew about Jane's case.

The staff at the Texas/Dallas History and Archives Division of Dallas' J. Erik Jonsson Library informed me further. Librarian Gary Jennings produced a volume of district court records, which preserves the tragic case of the "State of Texas vs Jane, a Slave."

Dated May 16, 1853 is this: "We the jury find the defendant guilty of murder in the first degree. We further find that the defendant is a slave of the value of seven hundred dollars and that the owner of the defendant has done nothing to evade or defeat the execution of the law upon said defendant. (signed) D.R Cameron, foreman."

And on May 17 the entry reads: "…And it being demanded of said Jane if she had anything to say why judgment and sentence of death should not there be passed upon her and the said Jane saying nothing thereto: It is therefore ordered adjudged and decreed by the court that the sheriff of Dallas County keep the said Jane in close confinement in the common jail of Dallas County until Friday the 27th of the present month of May, and that…between the hours of eleven o'clock a.m. and three o'clock p.m. the sheriff…take said Jane from the common jail of said county and convey her to a gallows erected for that purpose and there…hang the said Jane by the neck until she is dead…"

In an unpublished 1940 manuscript, *WPA Dallas Guide and History*—written by the Texas Writers' Project of the Works Projects Administration—is this paragraph:

"It was in 1853 that the first legal execution took place in the county. This was the hanging of Jane Elkins, a slave who had murdered a man named Wisdom at Farmers Branch. After a trial before Judge John H. Reagan, most notable jurist of his time, the woman was hanged May 27, 1853."

In an 1892 publication, *Memorial and Biographical History of Dallas County, Texas*, W.P. Overton, 71, who'd come to Dallas County in 1844, was quoted:

"The first legal hanging was in 1853 or 1854. A negress was executed for knocking a man in the head with an ax at Cedar Springs. He had hired her and she murdered him while he was asleep. I can't recall their names."

Overton's fuzzy memory can be forgiven. Nearly everyone forgets Jane.

END NOTES

References cited with explicit and implicit permission and also those with acknowledgments under the Law of Fair Use.

1. Parker, S.G. "The Faces & Voices of Recovery Campaign Raises Awareness About Recovery from Addiction: Strengthening and Sustaining the Faces & Voices of Recovery Coalition." Robert Wood Johnson Foundation. Retrieved December 13, 2012, from http://www.rwjf.org. Reproduced with permission of the Robert Wood Johnson Foundation, Princeton, N.J.

2. Exodus 20:5. *The Holy Bible*, King James Version (KJV).

3. When interviewed, almost half of the female prison population in this country reported that they had been "physically or sexually molested" prior to incarceration. Of those state prisoners who grew up with a parent who used drugs and/or alcohol, over three-fourths of the women reported abuse. Also, state prisoners who reported abuse were more likely to commit a violent crime. Wolf Harlow, Caroline. "Prior Abuse Reported by Inmates and Probationers" (NCJ-172879). U.S. Dept. of Justice. Retrieved May 2011 from http://www.bjs.gov/content/pub/press/parip.pr.

4. Matthew 23:37. (KJV).

5. II Corinthians 1:4. New International Version (NIV). Grand Rapids: Zondervan House, 1984.

6. Registered Trademark. Marathon Pharmaceuticals, LLC. Northbrook, IL 60062.

7. "Dolls," slang for any barbiturate or downer, derived from the movie *Valley of the Dolls* appearing in 1967 and taken from the 1966 book of the same name by Jacqueline Susann.

8. Communication with Evan Greenspan, May 2012. Greenspan's. 3405 Tweedy Boulevard, South Gate, CA 90280; www.greenspans.com.

9. Spanish slang for marijuana.

10. CRC opened in 1928 as the Lake Norconian Club, a luxury hotel. During the month following Pearl Harbor, President Franklin Roosevelt turned the resort into a naval hospital. The hospital closed and reopened several times before 1962. After that, the federal government donated the facility to the state to use as a narcotics center. Later, in the 1980s, felons were accepted to ease overcrowding in the prison system. CDCR-California Rehabilitation Center (CRC). "Special Historical Notes." Retrieved June 2011 from http://www.cdcr.ca.gov/ Facilities Locator/ SQ-Special_Notes.html.

11. LSD is an abbreviation for lysergic acid diethylamide, a psychedelic drug belonging to the ergoline family. It is non-addictive and infamous for its

psychological effects, such as visions and an altered sense of time. Users who have experienced flashbacks report that they are often unpleasant. *Wikipedia.* Retrieved May 2011 from http://en.wikipedia.org/wiki/Lysergic_acid_diethylamide.

12. Cannabinol, CBN, is one of some eighty-plus currently known cannabinoids found in the cannabis plant (marijuana). Individual cannabinoid compounds have "cannabi" in their nomenclature. Each has different pharmaceutical properties. Those derived naturally from the plant itself rather than from formulation are properly termed phytocannabinoids. Most noteworthy is that known as Delta-9-tetrahydrocannabinol, THC, the active ingredient in marijuana (Cannabinoid, Wikipedia, http://en.wikipedia.org/ wiki/Cannabinoid, accessed November 1, 2014). THC is an agonist for the CB1 receptors, which, in the simplest explanation, says THC affects the brain— the "desired effect" for its users. In contrast, CBN works on the CB2 receptors—it affects the immune system, the liver, the spleen, etc. Compared to THC, CBN has weak psychoactive properties. It has been found to be beneficial in the treatment of sleep disorders such as sleep apnea (Carley, David W, et al., U.S. Patent 7,705,039 (April 8, 2002); Carley, David W, et al., U.S. Patent 8,207,230 (December 4, 2009)); as an analgesic and anti-inflammatory agent in liniment form (Wallace, Walter H., U.S. Patent 6,949,582 (September 13, 2002)); and its derivatives in the treatment of HIV and certain tumors (Travis, Craig R., U.S. Patent 7,105,685 (September 12, 2006); "Cannabis and Cannabinoids," National Cancer Institute, http://www.cancer.gov/cancer-topics/pdq/cam/cannabis/healthprofessional/page4, accessed November 1, 2014. All phytocannabinoids, including THC, form through an enzyme-catalyzed reaction. Cannabinol, however, does not. It occurs from the aging of THC through exposure to ultraviolet light, heat, and oxygen. In general, CBN comprises less than one percent of the phytocannabinoids found in a plant. It is unusual that this pure form was available on the streets in the 1970s. Sensi, Seshata. "Cannabinoid Science 101: Cannabinol." Retrieved September 22, 2011, from http://sensiseeds.com/en/blog/cannabinoid- science-101-cannabinol/.

13. San Quentin State Prison sits on a site noted in an 1850 U.S. Coast Survey as "Puenta de Quentin" or Point San Quentin. The name stems from a Native American chief, although the spelling and pronunciation have deteriorated with history. Built in 1852, it enjoys the reputation of California's oldest prison. San Quentin was built to replace the prison ship Waban anchored in the San Francisco Bay that came ashore on Bastille Day, July 14, 1852, with forty to fifty convicts. Hence, the prison nickname of Bastille by the Bay. San Quentin State Prison. Special Historical Notes. Retrieved June 2, 2014, from http://www.cdcr.ca.gov/Facilities_Locator/SQ-Special_Notes.html.

14. Methadone is a synthetic opioid similar to morphine. It has similar effects to heroin without the "high" and thus finds use for alleviating the pain of withdrawal. Methadone is an oral medication with a long duration effect. Drug Information

Online, Methadone. Retrieved December 20, 2014, from http://www.drugs.com/ search.php?searchterm=methadone.

15. Hoch, Edward Wallis. (1849-1925). Seventeenth Governor of Kansas. "…that it hardly behooves any of us, to talk about the rest of us." Wikipedia. Retrieved June 2011 from http://www.wikipedia.org.

16. Proverbs 26:11. KJV. "As a dog returneth to his vomit, so a fool returneth to his folly."

17. *Easyriders Magazine.* Paisano Publications, LLC. 28210 Dorothy Drive, Agoura Hills, CA 91301.

18. PCP often appears on lists as a hallucinogen, but it is indeed an anesthetic, the purpose for which it was developed. It does, however, produce hallucinations along with frequent bizarre behavior. It is addictive. Legal manufacture stopped in 1960. Reports indicate that PCP produces bizarre mood disorders, paranoia, schizophrenia, violence, and amnesia. Other than the misnomer of Angel Dust, street names include Hog, Lovely, Wack, Ozone, Embalming Fluid, and Rocket Fuel. Drug Information Online, PCP. Retrieved July 15, 2011, from http://www. drugs.com/illicit/pcp.html.

19. State Execution Rates. Death Penalty Information Center. Retrieved December 1, 2011, from http://www.deathpenaltyinfo.org/state- execution-rates.

20. Carson, E. Ann, Golinelli, Daniela. "Prisoners in 2012: Trends in Admissions and Releases 1991-2012." Bureau of Justice Statistics. Retrieved February 2, 2013, from http://www.bjs.gov/ index.cfm?ty=pbdetail&iid=4842.

21. Charles Manson. Wikipedia. Retrieved January 12, 2012, from http:// en.wikipedia.org/wiki/Charles_Manson.

22. Statistical studies and inferences continue to increase on the violent behavior of those on PCP, and certainly more studies are needed. Early studies from the 1980s, such as those by Brecher[a] and Wish,[b] conclude that there is no distinct correlation between PCP and violent behavior. Studies by those such as Fauman,[c] on the other hand, show that PCP induces those who are normally quiet to become quieter and those normally aggressive to become more aggressive and appears to increase violent tendencies when mixed with other drugs and/or alcohol. McCardle's[d] data suggests that human aggression under PCP is "associated with certain personality traits and background features." The NIDA states in a revised 2009 report:[e] "While intoxicated, PCP abusers may become violent or suicidal and are, therefore, dangerous to themselves and others."

(a)Brecher, M; Wang, B.W.; Wong, H; and Morgan, J.P., "Phencyclidine and Violence: Clinical and Legal Issues, Journal of Clinical Psychopharmacology," 8(6), 397–401, Dec. 1988, Abstract, http://www.ncbi.nlm.nih.gov/ pubmed/3069880, Accessed 3/14/2012.

(b)Wish, E.D., "PCP and Crime: Just Another Illicit Drug?, National Institute for Drug Abuse (NIDA) Research Monograph Series," 64, 174–189, 1986, Abstract, https://www.ncjrs.gov/App/Publications/abstract.aspx?ID=162181, Accessed 3/14/2012.

(c)Fauman, B.J. and Fauman, M.A., "Phencyclidine Abuse and Crime: A Psychiatric Perspective, Bulletin of the AAPL," Vol10, No. 3, 171–176, 1982, Abstract, https://www.ncjrs.gov/App/Publications/abstract.aspx?ID=162166, Accessed 3/14/2012.

(d)McCardle, L. and Fishbein, D.H., "The Self-Reported Effects of PCP on Human Aggression, Addictive Behaviors," Volume 14, Issue 4, 1989, 465–472, Abstract, http://www.ncbi.nlm.nih.gov/pubmed/2782129, Accessed 3/14/2012.

(e)National Institute on Drug Abuse (NIDA), DrugFacts: Hallucinogens - LSD, Peyote, Psilocybin and PCP, Revised 2009, http://www.drugabuse.gov/publications/drugfacts/ hallucinogens-lsd-peyote-silocybin-pcp, Accessed 3/14/2012.

23. The Walls Unit is an *a propos* nickname for the Texas Department of Criminal Justice penitentiary known as the Huntsville State Prison. The name must come from the surrounding walls constructed in 1849 to a thickness of two to three feet. It is the oldest prison in Texas and was the last prison remaining in the former Confederate States of America after the Civil War. The Texas Prison Museum, located nearby in downtown Huntsville, Texas, houses Old Sparky, an electric chair, from bygone days at the Walls Unit. Old Sparky, resting in a separate alcove, is a high-backed, wooden chair polished to a noticeable luster, possibly from the perspiration of the condemned. Leather restraints on the arms and on a backing board at the feet anchor the prisoner to metal contacts; a thick wire ascends behind the chair to an attachable metal helmet. Ironically, the inmates themselves constructed Old Sparky, which would claim the lives of 362 condemned men between 1924 and 1964. All executions, male and female, still take place in the Huntsville Unit. The unclaimed bodies of the executed and of those who died from other causes rest in Joe Byrd Cemetery, otherwise known by the inmates as Peckerwood Hill. Retrieved April 15, 2012, from http://en.wikipedia.org/wiki/Huntsville_Unit.

24. James Willett, former warden of the Walls Unit and now director of the Texas Prison Museum, states in an article about the cemetery that, "The term 'peckerwood' refers to those inmates who were poor." Willett, James. Captain Joe Byrd Cemetery. Retrieved June 25, 2014, from http://www.txprisonmuseum.org/articles/cemetery.html.

25. Sergeev, Alexey. December 29, 2011. Peckerwood Hill Cemetery. Huntsville Texas Prison. Retrieved May 11, 2012, from http://www.asergeev.com/pictures/k/Huntsville_Texas_prison.htm.

26. The Goree Unit of TDCJ was originally the Goree State Farm for Women named after Thomas J. Goree, a Texas prison superintendent, and was established in 1911. It remained a women's prison until the early 1980s when it converted to a men's prison. Female prisoners then moved to the Mountain View Unit in Gatesville. Females on Death Row at Mountain View move into the Goree Unit on the day prior to their execution at the Huntsville Unit. Goree Unit. Wikipedia.

Retrieved May 2011 through February 2012 from http://en.wikipedia.org/wiki/Goree_Unit.

27. "Anon, Texas Department of Corrections - 30 Years of Progress; Texas Dept of Corrections." Box 99 Huntsville TX 77340. Retrieved April 15, 2012, from https://www.ncjrs.gov/App/Publications/ abstract.aspx?ID=44533.

28. Dilaudid is a prescription name for hydromorphone, a semi-synthetic opioid derived from morphine with a street name of Dillies. Usually injected, it is highly addictive and up to ten times more potent than morphine and up to five times more than heroin. (Trade name: Dilaudid®; street names: Dust, Juice, Smack, D, Footballs.) Drug Enforcement Administration, Office of Diversion Control, Drug & Chemical Evaluation Section, July 2013. Retrieved August 11, 2012, from http://www.deadiversion.usdoj.gov.

29. Dilaudid. Wikipedia. Retrieved August 11, 2012, from http://en.wikipedia.org/wiki/ Hydromorphonem.

30. Penal Code, Title 5. "Offenses Against the Person." Chapter 19, *Criminal Homicide*. Retrieved August 15, 2012, from http://www.statutes.legis.state.tx.us/Docs/PE/htm/PE.19.htm.

31. Original Indictment. Harris County District Clerks Office. Filed March 6, 1980.

32. Elavil (no longer available under this name in the U.S.) is an antidepressant, chemically known as amitriptyline HCl. A dosage of 150 mg per day is the recommended maximum, whereas a dosage of 300 mg is only for hospitalized patients. The noted dosage of Valium, however, appears to be low.

Elavil. Wikipedia. Retrieved February 4, 2012, from http://en.wikipedia.org/wiki/Amitriptyline.

33. Amitriptyline. Retrieved February 4, 2012, from http://www.nlm.nih.gov/medlineplus/druginfo/meds/a682388.html.

34. Brook, Daniel. "When God Goes to Prison." *Legal Affairs.* Retrieved November 4, 2014, from http://www.legalaffairs.org/issues/May-June-2003/feature_brook_mayjun03.msp.

35. Carol Vance Unit. Wikipedia. Retrieved November 4, 2014, from, http://en.wikipedia.org/Carol_Vance_Unit.

36. Phillips, Scott. "Racial Disparities in Capital Punishment: Blind Justice Requires a Blindfold." *America Constitution Society for Law and Policy.* October 2008. Retrieved December 27, 2014, from https://www. acslaw.org/publications/issue-briefs/racial-disparities-in-capital-punishment-blind-justice-requires-a-blindf-0.

37. Bryce, Robert. "Justice, Texas-style." Salon Media Group, Inc., June 9, 1999. Retrieved December 10, 2014, from, http://www.salon.com/1999/06/09/prosecutor/. This article first appeared in Salon.com at http://www.salon.com. An online version remains on the Salon archives. Reprinted with permission.

38. Horne, Andy, former assistant U.S. attorney, Harris County assistant district

attorney, 1967 and 1970. Personal communication, November 3, 2014.

39. Hebrews 13:2. KJV. "…some have entertained angels unawares."

40. "Teen Challenge came to Texas in 1968, with the opening of the San Antonio men's campus, then called the Westwood Center. Adult & Teen Challenge now operates three men's programs (San Antonio, Magnolia, Azle), two women's programs (Houston, San Antonio), a women and children's program (Houston), re-entry programs (Brenham, Houston, San Antonio), three thrift stores (Brenham, San Antonio, Fort Worth), and a referral office in Austin. This ministry, admitting over 350 students a year, continues to expand and offer hope to men and women with life-controlling addictions." Adult and Teen Challenge of Texas, Mission and History Statement. Retrieved April 23, 2012, from http://teenchallengetx.org/about-us/mission-history/.

41. Graham, Billy. 1954 Crusade. Billy Graham Evangelistic Associate Library. Retrieved May 25, 2012, from http://www.billygrahamlibrary.org.

42. Administrative Segregation or "Ad Seg" is "a status involving separation of an offender from the general population for the purpose of maintaining safety, security and order." *Offender Orientation Handbook.* Texas Department of Criminal Justice, November 2004, pg. 49. Retrieved May 1, 2012, from http://www.tdcj.state.tx.us/documents/Offender__Orientation_Handbook_English. pdf.

43. Romans 12:6-8. I Corinthians 12:4-11. Ephesians 4:8-11. KJV.

44. Markham, James W., Field, William T. "Gatesville State School for Boys." *Handbook of Texas Online.* Published by the Texas State Historical Association. Retrieved March 18, 2013, from http://www.tshaonline.org/handbook/online/articles/jjg02.

45. Field, William T. "Mountain View School for Boys." *Handbook of Texas Online.* Published by the Texas State Historical Association. Retrieved March 18, 2013, from http://www.tshaonline.org/handbook/online/articles/jjg02.

46. Josefa (Chipita) Rodriguez was convicted of murder in San Patricio de Hibernia, Texas, in 1863. She ran a rest stop of sorts, on the Welder ranch land on the Aransas River, furnishing travelers with meals and a cot on her porch. Reportedly she murdered John Savage with an ax for $600 in gold. Details are few regarding her arrest, conviction, and execution; even her name is suspect. During her trial, all she would say was "not guilty." Except for a week's transcripts, all court records were lost. In 1985, the 69th Texas State Legislature passed a resolution absolving Chipita Rodriguez of murder; Governor Mark White signed the resolution.

For many years, she was considered the first woman legally hanged in Texas, but this unfortunate honor belongs to Jane Elkins, a slave who was convicted of murder and legally hanged in Dallas, some ten years prior. Jane Elkins was a slave for a man named Wisdom, a widower who lived in Farmers Branch, a small community north of Dallas. She murdered him in 1852 with an ax as he lay sleeping. Interestingly, both females used an ax in their purported crimes. Jane's duties were to keep house and take care of Wisdom's children. The children were not harmed. Court records stated Jane's slave value at $700. She was legally hanged May 27, 1853.

Kent Biffle is a well-known Texas historian writing under the newspaper byline "Kent Biffle's Texana." *The Dallas Morning News* requested the reproduction of the entire article in Appendix B.

47. Penry, John Paul. Wikipedia. Retrieved March 26, 2013, from http://en.wikipedia.org/wiki.

48. Karla Faye Tucker. Wikipedia. Retrieved April 20, 2013, from http://en.wikipedia.org/wiki/Karla_Faye_Tucker.

49. Strom, Linda. "Karla Faye Tucker Set Free." *WaterBrook Multnomah,* (Random House). N.Y., 2000, 2006.

50. Hamilton Pool Park. Retrieved April 25, 2013, from https://parks.traviscountytx.gov/find-a-park/hamilton-pool.

51. Karla Faye Tucker photograph. Murderpedia. Retrieved May 1, 2013, from http://murderpedia.org/ female.T/t/tucker-karla-photos.htm.

52. Colossians 3:9-10. KJV.

53. II Corinthians 5:17. KJV.

54. Lowry, Beverly. *Crossed Over.* Knopf, N.Y., 1992.

55. Strom, Linda. "Karla Faye Tucker Set Free." *WaterBrook Multnomah,* (Random House). N.Y., 2000, 2006.

56. *The Pick Twelve Game.* An Interactive Jury Game, Texas Law-Related Education. Retrieved January 2, 2015, from http://texaslregames.org/games_web_eng/jury_game/index.html.

57. Williams, Calvin J. Retrieved May 10, 2013, from http://www.tdcj.state.tx.us/death_row/dr_offenders_no_ longer_on_dr.html.

58. Warden Plane was an excellent administrator, disciplinarian, and humanitarian. As previously noted, she redesigned the death row cells at Mountain View from animal cages to those more resembling dorm rooms. She passed away at age 98 in May 2013, during the writing of this chapter. Plane, Lucile Garrett. Retrieved May 14, 2013, from http://itemonline.com/obituaries/x730877037/Lucile-Garrett-Plane.

59. Kearl, Teresa. "The Weaver." Authorship is disputed to be by Grant Colfax Tullar or B.M. Franklin. U.S. Library of Congress, Washington DC, Card # 20060727210211. Retrieved October 18, 2014, from http://www.writersonthe-loose.com/writers/mk/index.cfm?story=32559.

60. Mike Barber Ministries. P.O. Box 6292, Kingwood, Texas 77325. Retrieved (nd) from http://pro-claim.tv.

61. Betty Beets home page. Canadian Coalition Against the Death Penalty. Retrieved May 15, 2013, from http://ccadp.org/bettiebeet.htm.

62. Betty Beets news update. Canadian Coalition Against the Death Penalty. Retrieved May 15, 2013, from http://ccadp.org/beetsnewsupdates.htm.

63. Philippians 2:12. KJV.

64. The Texas Ranger Hall of Fame and Museum interviewed Warden Plane in 2009 when she was in her 90s. She remembered Karla Faye and Pamela Perillo, although she got their crimes confused and misspelled Pamela's name when asked by the interviewer for its spelling. Ray, Nancy. Interview with Lucile Garrett Plane. Texas Ranger Hall of Fame and Museum. Retrieved April 7, 2009, from http://www.texasranger.org/E-Books/Oral%20History%20-Plane_Lucile_ Garrett.pdf.

65. "The Three-Gun-Monte." *Sack O' Fertilizer Conviction and Execution of Frances Elaine Newton,* November 2, 2010. Retrieved June 1, 2013, from http://www.skepticaljuror.com/2010/11/three-gun-monte-sack-o-fertilizer.html.

66. Dow, D.R., Tyler, J. Counsel for Frances Elaine Newton. Texas Innocence Network. *Ex parte* Frances Elaine Newton, Applicant. Application for Post-Conviction Writ of Habeas Corpus & Motion for Stay of Execution. 263rd Judicial District Court, Harris County, Texas. Retrieved May 15, 2013, from July 27, 2005.

67. Ibid.

68. Ibid.

69. Rimer, Sara, Bonner, Raymond. "Texas Lawyer's Death Row a Concern." *The New York Times,* June 11, 2000.

70. Ibid, 65.

71. State Bar of Texas. Find a Lawyer, Ronald G. Mock. Retrieved July 2013 from https://www.texasbar.com/AM/Template.cfm?Section=Find_A_Lawyer&template=/Customsource/MemberDirectory/.

72. Roosevelt, Franklin Delano, President. December 8, 1941.

73. David RUIZ et al., Plaintiff, United States of America, Plaintiff-Intervenor. W. J. ESTELLE, Jr., et al., Defendants. Civ. A. No. H-78-987. United States District Court, S. D. Texas, Houston Division, December 12, 1980. Retrieved July 22, 2013, from http:www.law.cornell.edu/supremecourt/text/426/925.

74. Ruíz v. Estelle. Wikipedia. Retrieved July 22, 2013, from http://en.wikipedia.org/wiki/Ruiz_v._Estelle.

75. Sagar, Kristen. "Ruíz v. Estelle." *The Civil Rights Clearing House.* University of Michigan Law School. Retrieved July 23, 2013, from http://www.clearinghouse.net/detail.php?id=960.

76. Perkinson, Robert, *Texas Tough, The Rise of America's Prison Empire,* Picador, Henry Holt & Company, New York, NY (2010).

77. White, Mark. Personal communication. December 12, 2013.

78. Smith, Jordan. "Prisoners' Rights Crusader Ruíz Dies." *The Austin Chronicle,* Nov. 25, 2005. Retrieved August 5, 2013, from http://www. austinchronicle.com/news/2005-11-25/313588/.

79. David Ruíz, Presente–1942-2005. "Heroes in Prison, TPNS." *Broken Chains.* Retrieved August 2, 2013, from http://brokenchains.us/tdcj/Heroes.html.

80. The final chapters of Ruíz v. Estelle. (*Judicial News*). The Free Library.

2002 American Correctional Association, Inc. Retrieved August 7, 2014, from http://www.thefreelibrary.com/The+final+chapter+of+Ruiz+Estelle.+(Judicial+News). -a087426102.

81. Legal Information Institute, LII. Free Legal Information for Everyone. Retrieved January 22, 2014, from http://www.Law.cornell.edu.

82. Walpin, Ned. "The New Speed-Up in Habeas Corpus Appeals." PBS, KERA 13. Retrieved January 26, 2014, from http://www.pbs.org/wgbh/pages/frontline/shows/execution/readings/texas.html.

83. Baker Botts L.L.P. One Shell Plaza, 910 Louisiana Street, Houston, Texas 77002.

84. Strom, Linda. "Karla Faye Tucker Set Free." *WaterBrook Multnomah,* (Random House). N.Y., 2000, 2006.

85. Arthur, Audrey. "For Better or For Worse: Proxy Marriages End Inmate Marriages in Texas." *Correctional News,* September 11, 2013. Retrieved February 1, 2014, from http://www.correctionalnews.com/article/11/better -worse-proxy-marriages-end-inmate-marriages-in-Texas.

86. HBO®, Home Box Office, Inc. A Division of Time Warner Inc. One Time Warner Center, New York, NY 10019-8016.

87. Michael Graczyk is a journalist with the Associated Press, who has become the AP's professional witness to executions and chronicles the subsequent articles. In this rather bizarre occupation, he has witnessed over 300 executions. Michael Graczyk. Wikipedia. Retrieved January 5, 2015, from http://en.wikipedia.org/wiki/Michael_Graczyk.

88. Robbins, Mary Alice. "Court Snuffs Out Challenge to Prison Smoking Ban." *Amarillo Globe News,* December 6, 1996. Retrieved October 8, 2013, from www.amarillo.com/stories/120696/snuffs.html.

89. Salvucci, Jessica. "Femininity and the Electric Chair: An Equal Protection Challenge to Texas's Death Penalty Statute." 31 B.C. Third World L.J. 405 (2011). Retrieved October 8, 2013, from http://lawdigitalcommons.bc.edu/twlj/vol31/iss2/7.

90. Matthew 26:39. NIV.

91. *Rhema,* from the Greek. "The Holy Spirit can cause certain passages to stand out with significant meaning or application for our lives. The Spoken Word of God, as one reads the Holy Scripture, enters one's heart via the Holy Spirit." Advanced Training Institute International. Retrieved November 1, 2014, from http://ati.iblp.org/ati/family/articles/concepts/rhema/.

92. Pamela Lynn Perillo, Petitioner-appellant, v. Gary L. Johnson, Director, Department of Criminal Justice, Institutional Division, Respondent-appelle. United States Court of Appeals, Fifth Circuit, 79 F.3d 441. March 21, 1996.

93. II Corinthians: 4:9. KJV.

94. Sister Helen Prejean is a well-known and vocal death penalty opponent who hails

from the Bayou State and has the Louisiana-French surname as well. She joined the Sisters of St. Joseph of Medaille (now the Congregation of St. Joseph) in 1957 when she was eighteen. After graduating from St. Mary's Dominican College in New Orleans, she obtained a Master in Religious Education from St. Paul's University in Ottawa, Canada. Following a career in education, she entered the prison ministry in 1981 when she became a pen pal with Patrick Sonnier, a Death Row inmate in Louisiana's Angola Prison. Angola has a nefarious history similar to that of the Walls Unit in Huntsville. From this experience, she wrote a book titled *Dead Man Walking: An Eyewitness Account of the Death Penalty.* The book was on the *New York Times* Best Seller List for thirty-one weeks and became an Oscar-nominated motion picture starring Susan Sarandon and Sean Penn. Sister Helen ministers to both the condemned and the murder victims' families and is the founder of Survive, a victim's advocacy group located in New Orleans. Appearing on many television and radio shows, she is a precious, inspired voice educating people about the death penalty and God's mercy and grace. Prejean, Helen, Sister. Retrieved November 1, 2013, from http://www.SisterHelen.org/biography/.

95. Bill Glass. "Champions for Life." Retrieved August 28, 2014, from http://www.billglass.org/ministries.htm.

96. *Larry King Live,* January 14, 1998. Transcript # 98011400V22. Retrieved December 1, 2013, from http://www.cnn.com/SPECIALS/1998/tucker.execution/transcripts/trans.1.14.html.

97. Prejean, Helen, Sister. *Death in Texas.* The New York Review of Books, January 13, 2005. Retrieved December 1, 2013, from http://www.nybooks.com/articles/archives/2005/jan/13/death-in-texas/.

98. "Last Meal." Wikipedia. Retrieved December 1, 2013, from http://en.wikipedia.org/wiki/Last_meal.

99. On September 21, 2011, Texas Death Row inmate Lawrence Russell Brewer, a white supremacist, faced execution for the hate crime of dragging James Byrd to death in Jasper, Texas. For his last meal, Brewer ordered: "two chicken-fried steaks, a triple-meat bacon cheeseburger, fried okra, a pound of barbecue, three fajitas, a meat-lover's pizza, a pint of ice cream, three root beers, and a slab of peanut butter fudge with crushed peanuts."

100. Then, he didn't eat any of it. Following an immediate outrage from the chairman of the State Senate Criminal Justice Committee, the TDCJ banned all last-meal requests. The condemned could eat what the other prisoners were eating. In reality, Brewer did not receive all that he requested. He, like all those before him, got "reasonable portions of foods already available in the prison's kitchen." Clarke, Matthew. "Texas Abolishes Last Meals for Death Row Prisoners, Reduces Weekend Meals." *Prison Legal News,* October 2012, p.28. Retrieved December 3, 2013, from www.prisonlegalnews.org/ news/2012/oct/15/texas-abolishes-last-meals-for-death-row-prisoners-reduces-weekend-meals/.

101. John 3:8. NIV.

102. Willett, James. Personal communication, August 19, 2014. Director, Texas Prison Museum, Huntsville, TX 77320.

103. Karla Faye Tucker, Offender Information. Retrieved December 6, 2013, from http://www.tdcj.state.tx.us/death_ row/dr_info/tuckerkarlalast.htm.

104. The Ellis Unit, TDCJ. Wikipedia. Retrieved December 7, 2013, from http://en.wikipedia.org/wiki/Ellis_Unit.

105. The Polunsky Unit, TDCJ. Wikipedia. Retrieved December 7, 2013, from http://en.wikipedia.org/wiki/Allan_B._Polunsky_Unit.

106. Perillo, Pamela. The Canadian Coalition Against the Death Penalty. Retrieved December 9, 2013, from http://ccadp.org.

107. Sworn Affidavit, 11/8/99. Alt.True-Crime. Retrieved January 15, 2014, from https://groups.google.com/forum/#!topic/alt.true-crime/CC-XZtdhdm0.

108. United States of America. Plaintiff-appelle versus Gilbert Martinez Musquia & Robert Martinez Gatewood, Defendants-appellants. United States Court of Appeals, Fifth Circuit, No. 93-2600, February 10, 1995. Retrieved (nd) from http://www.ca5.uscourts.gov/opinions/pub/93/93- 02600.CR0.wpd.pdf.

109. Prejean, Helen, Sister. *Death in Texas.* The New York Review of Books, January 13, 2005. Retrieved December 1, 2013, from http://www.nybooks.com/articles/archives/2005/jan/13/death-in-texas/.

110. Bill Glass. "Champions for Life." Retrieved October 28, 2014, from http://www.billglass.org/ministries.htm.

111. The Texas Board of Pardons and Paroles is not to be confused with the Texas Prison Board (created as the Texas Board of Criminal Justice in 1989). Texas Board of Criminal Justice. Retrieved January 31, 2014, from http://www.tdcj.state.tx.us/mediasvc/tbcj/index.html.

112. Also in 1989, the Board of Pardons and Paroles was revamped to include eighteen members. The governor nominates the members of both entities, and obviously each must mirror his ideology. Lucko, Paul M. "Texas Prison System." *Handbook of Texas on Line.* Published by the Texas State Historical Association. Retrieved January 31, 2013, from http://www.tshaonline.org/ handbook/online/articles/mdbjq.

113. Lucko, Paul M. "Board of Pardons and Paroles." *Handbook of Texas on Line.* Published by the Texas State Historical Association. Retrieved February 3, 2014, from http://www.tshaonline.org/ handbook/online/articles/mdbjq.

114. Farewell Letter from Betty Beets—on the Eve of Her Execution. Retrieved January 4, 2014, from http://ccadp.org/finalbettie.html.

115. Ibid, 102.

116. Romans 13:4. NIV.

117. Recinella, Dale S. *The Biblical Truth About America's Death Penalty.* Northeastern University Press, 2014.

118. Correspondence with Joe Margulies regarding: The Execution of Betty Lou Beets, Reprieve, http://www.reprieve.org.uk/blog2012_10_10_PUB_margulies_execution_Betty_wdadp/, Accessed 2/14/2014. Link reported to be broken. See Joseph Margulies, Memories of an Execution, 20 U. Minn. J. of Law & Inequality 125 (Winter 2002).

119. Application for Reprieve from Execution of Death Sentence and Commutation of Sentence for Imprisonment for Life, http://www.webfaerie.com/content/WI_Archive/library/reference/bl_beets_cl.htm, Accessed 1/10/2015.

120. Joseph Margulies, http://www.lawschool.cornell.edu/faculty/bio.cfm?id-369, Accessed 1/10/2015.

121. The Ministry Church. Retrieved February 6, 2014, from http://www.theministrychurch.org/.

122. Betty Beets News Update. Canadian Coalition Against the Death Penalty. Retrieved February 6, 2014, fromhttp://ccadp.org/beetsnewsupdates.htm.

123. Ibid, 118.

124. Ibid, 118.

125. Carlin, Paul Dr. Personal communication, February 13, 2014.

126. Ibid.

127. Merle Haggard. "If We Make It Through December 1973." Retrieved March 2, 2014, from http://en.wikipedia. org/wiki/If_We_Make_It_ Through_December.

128. Plane State Jail. Retrieved March 4, 2014, from http://www.tdcj.state.tx.us/unit_ directory/lj.html.

129. Ibid, 58.

130. Hilltop Unit. Retrieved April 4, 2014, from, http://www.tdcj.state.tx.us/unit_directory/ht.html.

131. Genesis 4: 15. KJV.

132. "Frances Newton." Wikipedia. Retrieved May 7, 2014, from http://en.wikipedia.org/wiki/Frances_ Newton.

133. Strom, Linda. "Karla Faye Tucker Set Free." *WaterBrook Multnomah,* (Random House). N.Y., 2000, 2006.

134. Philippians 4:17. (KJV).

135. Blackaby Ministries International. Retrieved August 2014 from http://www.blackaby.net.

136. "David Jeremiah." Retrieved August 2014 from http://www.davidjeremiah.org/site.

137. "Faith Based Dorm." *The Christian Broadcast Network.* Retrieved August 2014 from http://www.cbn.com/tv/1387654878001.

138. Acts 9:1-22. KJV.

139. Patriot PAWS Service Dogs. 254 Ranch Trail, Rockwall, TX 75032. Retrieved August 2014 from http://patriotpaws.org/prison-program/.

140. The ancient Greeks used two words for time: *chronos* for chronological

or sequential time and *kairos* for a special interval of time, often indistinct. So, *chronos* for quantitative time and *kairos* for qualitative time. In theology, *kairos* refers to a time when God acts. *Kairos.* (2014, May 27). *New World Encyclopedia.* Retrieved October 6, 2014, from http://www. newworldencyclopedia.org/p/index. php?title=Kairos&oldid=981846.

141. Kairos Prison Ministry International. Retrieved October 6, 2014, from http://kpmifoundation.org/index.php.

142. Emmaus was a small town near Jerusalem. According to Luke 24:13-35, two of Jesus's disciples were walking along the road to Emmaus after the crucifixion. They did not recognize the resurrected Christ until they reached Emmaus, sat down for supper with Him, and as He broke bread and blessed it, their eyes opened. In a *kairos* moment, they knew Him and He vanished. Luke 12:13. KJV.

143. "List of Deadly Women." The Discovery Channel. Retrieved October 6, 2014, from http://en.wikipedia.org/wiki/List_of_Deadly_Women_episodes.

144. Iniquity-Definition and Meaning. "Bible Dictionary." *Bible Study Tools.* Retrieved October 9, 2014, from http://www.biblestudytools.com/encyclopedias/isbe/iniquity.html.

145. "What Does Exodus 20:5 Mean?" *Spiritual Seeds.* Retrieved October 9, 2014, from http://spiritualseeds.weebly.com/the-true-meaning-of-exodus-205.html.

146. Fisher, G. Richard. "A Study in Evolving Fadism." *The Dangerous Leanings of Bill Gothard's Teachings,* Personal Freedom Outreach. Retrieved October 9, 2014, from http://spiritualseeds.weebly.com/the-true-meaning-of-exodus-205.html.

147. Calvary Commission. Retrieved November 11, 2014, from http://www.calvarycommission.org/prison/.

About the Author

John T. Thorngren, a Texas writer and graduate of the University of Texas, has enjoyed a myriad of life experiences, working from basements to boardrooms in such positions as a salesman for a chemical laboratory calling on sewage plants; an insurance agency secretary; liaison engineer stationed in Paris, France; retail store owner; computer programmer; machine shop owner; engineering consultant; retail inventory; fabrication design engineer; car wash soap manufacturer; electronic control manufacturer; chemical plant operator; oil field roustabout; financial consultant; and rental management. He is a songwriter published in Southern Gospel and an author of several patents, technical articles, and a nonfiction book on probability and statistics. John and his wife of more than five decades live in Shady Shores, Texas, on Lake Lewisville, where their livestock freely roam the grounds. After his first heart attack at an early age and two subsequent ones followed by two open-heart surgeries, he believes that God has a purpose for every life.